Navigating
Entrepreneurship

Navigating Entrepreneurship

11 Proven Keys to Success

Larry Jacobson

BEP BUSINESS EXPERT PRESS

Navigating Entrepreneurship: 11 Proven Keys to Success

First published in 2018 by
Business Expert Press, LLC
222 East 46th Street, New York, NY 10017
www.businessexpertpress.com

ISBN-13: 978-1-94819-855-4 (paperback)
ISBN-13: 978-1-94819-856-1 (e-book)

Business Expert Press Entrepreneurship and Small Business Management Collection

Collection ISSN: 1946-5653 (print)
Collection ISSN: 1946-5661 (electronic)

Cover and interior design by Exeter Premedia Services Private Ltd., Chennai, India

First edition: 2018

10 9 8 7 6 5 4 3 2 1

Printed in the United States of America.

Abstract

Success requires experience. You can either learn it the hard way—the school of hard knocks—or you can learn it from someone who's already been there. What's your time worth? Why not leverage your time by using Larry Jacobson's 20 years of experience? Larry's been an entrepreneur all of his life and in this book he shares the Keys to his success. He's lived it; he's the real deal. Through artfully written stories from his business career and sailing journey around the world, he shares practical wisdom easily applied to your life story. There's no "made up" or "researched" information here. This is the real thing from a successful entrepreneur. A nationally recognized thought leader, Larry's articles have appeared in Forbes, MSNBC, The Huffington Post, YAHOO! Finance, PBS, and more.

A sought after motivational speaker, Larry also coaches entrepreneurs. Because not everyone can hire him as a coach, he created this "nuts and bolts" book. You'll pick up his "whatever-it-takes" attitude of self-reliance and decisiveness, as well as new thinking about Leadership. It's no secret that knowledge is power. You move forward when you educate yourself, and this book is a fun way to add to your knowledge bank.

Keywords

attitude, challenges, commitment, decision making, entrepreneur, entrepreneurship, fear, goals, goal-setting, leadership, managing your fears, overcoming fears, perspective, perseverance, positive attitude, risk, solopreneurship, tenacity, vision, working alone

Contents

Introduction

Welcome Entrepreneurs!

Congratulations! This book will be one of the most important steps you take in your entrepreneurial life. Being an entrepreneur isn't easy, but the more you understand the emotions and feelings you are having, the easier the ride will be. Entrepreneurs are leaders by nature. The better your leadership skills, the easier the ride will be. And leadership starts with you. The following chapters will explore proven leadership keys to support your unstoppable success. Whether you are a solopreneur on the brink of your entrepreneurial journey, in management, or you have just been thrust into a leadership position, you will learn the skills, traits, and characteristics to exponentially improve your leadership skills and thus, the performance of your business. This book will provide you with all the necessary tools for weathering any storm you encounter as an entrepreneur. And that will mean not worrying about your rent or, perhaps, getting that new car or house. It might also mean having more funds to do good for others.

If you're in business, you have the entrepreneurial spirit. I've never met a businessperson who didn't have an entrepreneur inside of them. You are a leader, an explorer, one who defies the norm, pursues ideas, and follows YOUR passion, not that of someone else. These days, more and more people are starting their own small businesses and need leadership skills to manage themselves and others. And being a leader is becoming increasingly more important in the corporate world, as companies continue to seek those with leadership skills. Many companies are seeking independent thinkers like you because they want innovation, creativity, and the drive of the entrepreneurial spirit.

Some of you already have business experience, and some of you don't. Either way, you will learn to get the most out of every day; to enjoy the journey; and to live without fear, confident that you can lead yourself and others through anything the business world throws at you.

You'll learn that the same skills and traits used in business are the ones you'll use in your personal life to make your dreams come true. The 11 keys I'm about to share with you are proven. They are the same traits I used in my business career, and they are the very ones I used to make my dream come true—sailing my own boat around the world.

Let me be very clear. This book is not about me. It's about you learning the skills, traits, and characteristics I wish I had been more aware of during my business career. I listened to numerous audio programs and read scores of books, but none had in them the information I'm about to share with you. I often think, "If only I had this mindset when I was a young man in business." I guess that's why it's called experience—you can't get it unless you either live it, or learn it from someone who has.

I will share stories from my business life and from my sailing journey around the world. The conclusions and proof that we draw together from these stories will guide you to be a better leader. The Action Guide will make them stick.

What you learn here will help you be more productive than you are today. You'll gain more profits, more time, and you will learn the leadership skills needed to succeed in business. Additionally, what you learn will reduce stress in your business and personal life. Some people have the entrepreneurial spirit but are stressed because it can be overwhelming. They lack the ability to break their overwhelm into smaller parts that are more manageable. You're going to learn how to do that. This book will help you enjoy being an entrepreneur!

I speak from experience—a lot of experience. But to be clear: I'm just a regular guy who had a dream—of making it in business, and sailing around the world. I'm not Ernest Shackleton or Sir Edmund Hillary shaking my fist at the fury of the storm. I'm not Richard Branson or Felix Baumgarden rocketing into or jumping out of space to set a record. And I'm not a millionaire business tycoon with my own jet. I'm not much different than you are. I'm just a regular guy with dreams—big dreams. In order to make those dreams a reality, I realized early on that I had to chart a course, not just to get around the world, but to live my life in a way that would give me the results I was seeking. I believe that I can achieve anything I set my mind to. Somewhere along the line, someone told me that, and all I did was believe them. I'm now that someone telling YOU that YOU can achieve anything. Believe me.

The naysayers call me lucky. To them, I reply that luck is what you get when you combine **perspiration with good choices**. The keys you are about to learn will be the basis for your good choices. Sorry, you'll still have to do the work.

At age 13 when I learned to sail, I started dreaming of navigating my own boat all the way around the world. I achieved that dream by beginning my six-year circumnavigation 33 years after I first stepped foot in a sailboat. I learned a lot in those six years at sea. Realizing my dream of sailing around the world meant staying the same course I had charted in my prior successful business life. And it means the same living back on land. I will only remain captain of my own ship and my own destiny if I continue to live by the principles, the traits, the characteristics, and skills I'm about to share with you. Remember the quote by William Henley: "I am the master of my fate: I am the captain of my soul." Try saying that out loud, it feels SO good. "I am the master of my fate: I am the captain of my soul."

My first dream was success in business, and I achieved that over my 20-year career in the incentive travel and events management industry. I'm definitely an entrepreneur. I started with one desk, a telephone, and a phone directory. To start, I picked up the phone and started dialing. Twenty years later, our company had grown into the darling of the industry. We were known as the high-end leader. We beat out the large, well-established companies every time, and we never, ever, not even once, lost a client to a competitor. Our clients became raving fans. They never asked us to reduce our price, they never asked how much money we made, and they never questioned our advice. We were honest, gave more than we promised, provided impeccable service, and were always one step ahead of the big guys. Our employees never left. Our clients became our sales force and referred new business to us. We were a resounding success.

But even after great success in business, I found something to be missing. I still had the burning desire of my childhood dream to sail around the world. To achieve that enormous goal, I used the same principles I used in business.

It hasn't been all roses though, and I have had my business failures, but without failure, success doesn't taste so sweet. I've started a couple of businesses that have not met my expectations, goals, and objectives. I've lost my shirt more than once. That's one of the risks of entrepreneurship. There are no guarantees. That's why you're reading this book, so you can be the best-prepared possible.

While sailing, I've run aground, hit a rock, nearly lost the mast, got caught in big storms, misread weather charts, and made mistakes fixing mechanical problems. But I made it all the way around the world and I owe that success to the traits and characteristics I'm going to share with you in this book.

I now have a new goal: To help entrepreneurs like you. It's time to share my knowledge, to give back, and to help you avoid potential pitfalls. It's worth repeating: it's not a coincidence that the same skills and traits you're about to learn apply equally to your business and your personal life. Call it a bonus. You don't have to learn two different sets of keys; they are the same. These keys are not secrets. They are not in code, and they are easily within your reach every single day ... because they are inside of you! You don't have to sail all the way around the world to learn that

Your Unstoppable Success is inside of YOU.

What Others Are Saying

Navigating Entrepreneurship is an inspiring journey to personal and business success. The 11 keys are filled with specific advice on dealing with challenges and fears as well as proven strategies for goal attainment.

Written and spoken by the author in a heartfelt and dynamic style, it will surely be of great value for any entrepreneur looking to leap to the next level.

—Mitch Meyerson, Author of 11 Business Books

Funny, witty, charming, and most of all, a hard-hitting leader who allows no excuses because he provides the answers.

—G.W. McDonald, Attorney

Finally, a very practical program that goes beyond just theory—Larry Jacobson delves into the depths and demonstrates clearly, yet simply, how you too can become successful!

—Andre Hodgskin, Architectural Corporation Director

I was focused on the wrong things.
Now my priorities are clear and I'm moving forward.

—Robert Schnell, Artist and Gallery Owner

Larry gave me the confidence I needed to move in my new career direction.

—Gary Saylor, Marine Business Owner

He was speaking right to me! How did he know what I was going through? It's like he was reading my mind. Just when I was about to say, "What about …," there he was with the next section answering my question.

—Laurie Nilson, Start-up Entrepreneur

Larry's amazing at getting me focused on what's important. If you can't hire Larry as your personal coach, this book is your next best ally.

—Raul Valadao, Teacher

With the art of a true storyteller, Larry Jacobson weaves his important points about leadership with his experience as an entrepreneur and at sea. His points are clear and well presented. A must read for every entrepreneur!

—Dave Talton, Mortgage Broker

CHAPTER 1

How Leadership Meets the Challenges of Being an Entrepreneur

Leadership is not just an ability to guide others. You will be a better leader of others if you know how to guide yourself, so that's what we will focus on first. Let's start by talking about you and your challenges. Let me ask you some questions.

1. Do you dream of big things, great ideas, and accomplishing extraordinary goals? Then, just as quickly, do you "check" yourself? Do you think, "I could never do that?" Have you identified your core ambitions and what lights your fire? If you haven't, you're not alone. It doesn't just happen passively. If you haven't identified your dreams, go to my website now and take the free passion quiz. It will help you while you read this book when I refer to your big dream. You'll find the quiz at: http://larryjacobson.com/passion-quiz/

2. Do you turn your dreams into goals? If you have big dreams, they can be daunting. When you break down big dreams into smaller achievable goals, suddenly they don't seem so formidable. I will help you through this process.

3. Have you ever felt that your current life and identity are holding you back from moving on to a different life of which you've always dreamed? Are you afraid of letting go of certain things in order to move on to the next?

4. Do you have difficulties making decisions? Once you decide something, do you stick to it?

5. Do you experience fear of moving forward in some key areas of your business or personal life? Are you comfortable with change?

6. Speaking of fears, what are you afraid of? Every entrepreneur experiences fear. It's part of the deal. It's a matter of deciding who is in charge, you or your fears? You will learn how to use your fears to your advantage. Yes, your fears will be working **for** you!

7. A common question I'm asked is, "how can I be an effective leader of my entrepreneurial venture, and a leader of others, if I don't know what I'm doing?" Here's the good news: You don't have to know what you're doing. I'm living proof of this. I think you may be surprised by how little many entrepreneurs knew before they began their ventures.

8. When working toward completion of a project, do you run out of steam? Do you wish you had more perseverance?

9. Do you ever wonder how to earn instant respect from coworkers and clients? Here's a hint: you have two ears and only one mouth for a reason.

Have you noticed that these questions are about you? They're about how to lead you. Next, you will learn the keys to leading others. I will share from my 20 years of experience, the most important elements of leading and motivating others. You will use all of what you learned about leading yourself, plus several new skills with which to lead others.

Last question: do you know the number one key to being a successful entrepreneur and leader? Don't worry, you will by the end of the book.

If the questions resonated with you, you're not alone. I know what you're going through because I faced the same issues.

Your background, financial status, geographic location, political affiliations, and age make no difference. What DOES make a difference is what you do to affect your life from **this day forward**. By simply reading this book, you've made a decision to improve your skills, which will improve your overall life. I learned these Keys the hard way—through 20 years of business, and more than 50,000 miles of sailing—so these ideas are **Boardroom and Ocean-tested**. By the end of this book, you'll know what it means to be **Unstoppable!** Ready? Let's tackle those questions.

Passion Quiz

These questions are designed to help you clarify what you love, what you are passionate about, and what you want to achieve in your life. Answer them honestly—only you will be looking at them. Be bold with your answers. Once completed, review your answers and notice patterns, similar responses, repeated words; they will likely lead you to your passion.

1. What makes you smile?
2. What makes you leap out of bed in the morning?
3. What are you doing when you feel invincible?
4. What do people thank you for most often?
5. On what subject(s) do people ask you for advice?
6. What are you really good at doing? What are your precious gifts?
7. Who do you look up to? Who are your mentors? Who inspires you? Why?
8. When was the last time you over-delivered on something? What was it, and why did you work so hard?
9. When was the last time you were in a state of flow, in the zone and totally lost track of time? What were you doing?
10. Imagine that you won the lottery. How will you spend tomorrow?
11. What would you do if you knew you could not fail?
12. What topics do you find yourself continuously arguing or defending with others?
13. What are you most afraid of for the next generation, whether you have kids or not?
14. What do you love helping people with? How do you most commonly help others?
15. What's your favorite section in the bookstore? What's the first magazine you pick up at the newsstand?
16. When was the last time you couldn't sleep because you were so excited about what you were working on?
17. If you trusted that your art (your creativity) would support your life financially, how would you live? Richly, sparsely, where?
18. Of all your current work roles, what would you gladly do for free?

19. If you were able to attend your own funeral, what would you want to hear people say?

20. What do you want to be remembered for—what mark do you want to have put on the world?

21. What do your friends always tell you you'd be good at, that you should do for a living (i.e., "he'd make a great...")? If you don't remember, ask them.

22. What are you naturally curious about?

23. When you have a free hour to surf the Internet, what do you explore?

24. Think back to when you were 5 or 10 years old. What did you want to be when you grew up? Anything goes. What skills and metaphors do these represent (i.e., pilot may be a symbol for exploration)?

25. If you could write a book to help the world that is guaranteed to be a best seller, what would the title be? What's it about?

26. What careers do you dream about? What jobs do others have that you wish were yours?

27. What dream jobs or businesses can you imagine that would firmly embody your core beliefs about the world?

28. What revolution do you want to lead?

Here's to living with passion! Now that you know what your passion is, decide to pursue it!

Ralph Waldo Emerson said, "Once you make a decision, the universe conspires to make it happen."

Let the universe help you! Don't deny your passion; don't turn away from it. Don't let fear or any other obstacle stand in the way of it. Embrace your passion, get energized about it, and use your passion as a tool of strength!

Larry Jacobson

www.LarryJacobson.com

CHAPTER 2

Why You Should Stare Out the Window and Dream

Let's start by breaking the myth about what many people see as idle dreaming. I believe those who dream have a better chance of achieving great success because they're able to dream, to see, to envision things that don't yet exist. Some people think dreaming is a waste of time, but that's not true. Dreaming of success is the first step to success. Of course, you can't just dream, there's more to it. I've had plenty of dreams that didn't amount to a hill of beans, that went nowhere, including companies that didn't make it. In hindsight, I don't think I was dedicated to those dreams. I couldn't see them; I couldn't see me doing what I was dreaming about. I dreamt about it, but I **didn't see me in the dream and that made all the difference.**

You must envision yourself in your dreams.

Do you have a dream? Is it big? Make it big! Set your sights higher! This can be a personal dream or a business dream, or maybe your personal dream is of business success. You can dream of a happy family vacation or being CEO in a penthouse office overlooking the city. For example, I dreamt the same dream for 30 years. I wanted to sail around the world on my own boat. When I closed my eyes, I saw myself standing behind the wheel of my own sailboat gliding out the Golden Gate. If I kept my eyes closed, I saw myself sitting on a white sand beach under a swaying palm tree, in front of a turquoise blue bay, while feeling the warm tropical trade winds on my skin. And if I kept my eyes closed long enough, and kept the vision in my mind, I could see myself sailing back underneath the Golden Gate Bridge after sailing around the world. My vision was so clear I could see friends and family standing on the Golden Gate Bridge cheering. I could see boats coming out to greet us; I could see dozens of people standing on the dock cheering; and I could see champagne corks flying. And, guess what? That is exactly the way it happened. Close your eyes. What do you see?

During my 20-year business career, before giving a presentation for a million dollar sale, I could see and hear the client nodding and asking the right questions. I could see shaking hands and saying, "It's a pleasure working with you. I'll have the agreement drawn up and sent to you today." Watch an Olympic skier standing at the top of their run. They close their eyes and they see themselves going down the run, making every turn perfectly, and finishing in record time. Close your eyes again. Now what do you see?

What you see in your dreams, your vision, doesn't have to be sailing around the world or climbing Mt. Everest. In fact, most people think the dream of sailing around the world is crazy. Heck, even my mother thought it was crazy! You might see having a home-based business that you operate from your kitchen table so you can be with your kids. It's relative only to you, and no one else. It's only **your** dream that's important right now.

Helen Keller said, "Life is either a daring adventure, or nothing." But it's not just doing daring things that make your life an adventure. Your life is just as big an adventure as mine or anybody else's. In fact, to you it's bigger, and certainly the most important.

What can you "see" yourself doing? When you visualize, you must be able to put yourself in the picture. I could smell the breeze, feel the sand beneath my feet, and get as excited as if I was really sailing. Feel and see yourself crossing the finish line to your dream. The passion you feel is key. This will be an important anchor for you throughout this program because passion wins out over everything else, including fear. **What do you see when you close your eyes? If you can see it, you can do it. If you can see it, then you can say it. And if you can say it, then you can write it down.**

What do you dream about? What's your core? What makes you leap out of bed in the morning without a cup of coffee? What keeps you up too late at night and wakes you up too early in the morning? What drives you? Is it art? Helping people? Being salesman of the year? Climbing Mt. Everest? Rise to the occasion and become a super-hero obligating yourself to the core. There's a super-hero inside each of you. But like the song by M People says, "You have to search for the hero inside yourself." Nobody else is going to do it for you.

If you're unsure of your dreams, ask yourself some questions to spark your thinking. For example:

- What do you speak about with passion? Do you have a small business directed toward helping Moms in a small way, or do you want to take over the Mommy industry?
- What makes you smile? Being a small-time operator working from home or a penthouse office on Park Avenue?
- What makes you all warm and fuzzy inside? Helping others or making oodles of money?
- Don't forget to include your personal dreams. What are your hobbies, passions, and personal values? If you really don't know what your passions are, what you truly love, then take the Passion Quiz. It's free, all you have to do is go to my website and download it at http://larryjacobson.com/passion-quiz/
- What title do you see on your business card?
- What income would you like?
- What is your BIG Dream?

I just mentioned this, but it's so important that I'm going to mention it again now, and later. If you can say it, then you can write it. Write it down. Add the details, see the vision, and believe in what you see. See yourself making this dream come true. Where do you write this down?

In the ACTION GUIDE of course. You'll find the action guide at http://larryjacobson.com/action-guide/. You can fill it in on your computer, or print it and work with it manually. You'll also find it in the back of this book. You can use it over and over again. Rework it until it reflects what you want in your future. You'll see the place to write down your big dream. Put in some details: the sand dripping between your toes, the stockholders applauding their CEO, you name it.

Remember from this chapter that Effective Leaders are Dreamers. You now have your dream written on paper. It's a big first step.

.

CHAPTER 3

Turning Dreams Into Goals

All effective leaders use visioning to see themselves achieving their dreams and goals, which brings us to the difference between dreams and goals. Some of your dreams may be big, **really** big. Too big? Nope, they're never too big. But, sometimes they seem overwhelming, so we're going to take the next step and break your dreams down into smaller achievable goals and make them less overwhelming.

How about we start with why? Why do you have to break your big dream down into goals? Because a dream is just that—a dream—until you transform it into a goal. You can make a dream come true, and the easiest way to do that is to see it not only as a dream but also as a goal. When you see your dream as a big goal made up of smaller goals, it seems more achievable. Then upon putting the small goals back together, you see you can achieve any goal, no matter how big. I'm not a big fan of sports metaphors but football surely fits here. When you get that ball to a first down, you get another chance to go again. You don't have to run the entire 100 yards at once. In baseball, you just need to reach one base at a time. You can sail around the world one island or country at a time, and you can write a book one chapter at a time.

Goals can be seen, identified, and talked about, but they must be written down. Why? Because writing your goals helps to keep you on track and accountable. I still have the piece of paper that I wrote my goals on 10 years before sailing out the Golden Gate. On that paper, I had two things listed for my personal goals 10 years down the road. The first was to own a 50 foot sailboat and cruise the islands of the Pacific. The boat I sailed away on was 50 feet and I not only cruised the Pacific, but also continued on all the way around the world. The second goal was to honor my mother in a significant way. I named my boat after her and sailed JULIA all the way around the world. Writing down your goals works. So let's get specific about goal setting and make it work for YOU. Let's start with three broad steps.

1. First of all, it helps to know what you want. You know what happens when you go to the grocery store without a list. You come home with lots of things, but you may have forgotten the milk. Have you ever gone to Costco without a list? I can hear you laughing because we've all done that and come home with hundreds of dollars of items that we may or may not have needed.
2. After you know what you want, the second step is to make a plan.
3. Thirdly, you'll work your plan.

OPEN YOUR ACTION GUIDE, and let's get to work. You'll find the action guide at http://larryjacobson.com/action-guide/ and at the back of this book. This is the longest section in the Action Guide, but it's important because it builds your foundation. Let's try to help you figure out what you want and let's do it by category:

Financial

How much money do you want to make, what investments would you like, what about real estate, savings?

Personal

What would you like to see in a Relationship? Maybe you don't have one, and want one. Maybe you're in one, and want to get out. What about your health such as your weight, eating habits, and exercise? Don't forget the material things you want such as a beach house, sailboat, new car, new set of dishes, and a bicycle?

Career

Are you Happy? Do you want a new direction? What about a new promotion, switching to a new company, or starting a business? Sometimes Career and Financial overlap. If they do for you, that's fine. But for some, your current career doesn't coincide with your financial goals. Only you can assess that.

Now look at the timeframe for each category and each goal.

What do you want financially, personally, and career-wise over a period of:

- Six months
- One year
- Five years
- 10 years

Here are your Action steps: Don't complicate this, just do it. Once you've written down your goals, which can be one word or longer, write down three action items needed to accomplish each goal. This may take a bit of time, so be patient but keep at it. Really think out each step and write them down. These can include things you need to do, people you need to help you, or skills you need to learn. For example, if you want to write a book, but can't type, it might be helpful to learn, or to buy the software that translates your voice into the written word. You could record your book and send it to someone and they'll type it for you. There's more than one way to get something done! It's so easy to come up with reasons not to do things. Sometimes we have to tell ourselves: **No excuses.**

Now, sort these action items by their priority. We'll talk more about priorities later, but for now, just sort them with an A for higher priority, or put a gold star next to the item that needs to be done first. Whatever works for you and Keep it Simple!

NOW LET THE GOALS SIT on your desk for a day or two or three, but no more than three. Then look at them again and see what you think. Do you like them? Do they make your eyes light up and your heart sing? Or do they depress you? If they depress you, such as mine does, "Lose 15 pounds," then I'm going to adjust it to say, "Lose two pounds this month." And on my action item list, in order to lose those two pounds, I might say, "eliminate chocolate chip cookies for a month." Oh, did we have to say eliminate chocolate chip cookies … sigh. Anyway, do you see the difference? Two pounds is much more attainable and still takes me closer to my goal of 15 pounds. Most importantly, I feel better about achieving that smaller goal than not achieving a goal at all. Adjust your goals as you see fit, **making some attainable, and others a stretch.**

With the detail you've just created to achieve your goals, you now have a map (it's called a chart on a boat; so in case I say chart at some point, you'll know what I mean) to come back to when you get thrown off course. And you will get thrown off course. For example, all I can think about right now are chocolate chip cookies, and I have a feeling that I'm going to have one or two very soon. If I do have some cookies, I know that I will have to eliminate them for the rest of the month to compensate. I can see visibly in writing that they are not consistent with my goals and objectives. So I can get back on course.

Remember that storms happen at sea, and on land, and in life. Expect it and you won't be surprised because with your ACTION ITEM list, you will always know what the next thing is that you should do. And you created it. Nobody else. You are responsible only for YOU.

It's like your boat's course that you're charting. On board my boat, we had procedures for heavy weather, for sailing at night, and other situations. It made life easier. When nighttime came, we simply "rigged for night sailing." That meant checking the deck, checking lines, turning on lights, and other safety procedures. Remember that all of the things you're learning here are processes, not necessarily an event that will just happen. **Have some patience with yourself.** Follow these simple steps and you will learn to follow your goals just like I followed a course around the world. Now, I'm going to go have a cookie. Just kidding!

A word about TAKING ACTION: After you achieve an action item in each category, add a new action item. Keep going! You have to keep moving. Your life is like a boat, which can't be steered unless it's moving. The rudder is useless without water moving past it. Your life is like that— keep it moving. Keep doing something. When you finish one thing, move onto the next. Now, let's be clear: I'm not a taskmaster and I think it's important to pause sometimes, and give yourself some credit for items achieved. If you're on a scuba diving vacation, don't constantly worry about your next action item. Reward and recuperation are motivating. When you get back from your reward, whether it's a scuba diving vacation or a night out, that'll be soon enough to move onto the next action item.

Each action item that you achieve should be checked off as it's completed. This gives your brain a psychological boost that says, "See, I can make my goals happen!" You'll start to think of yourself as a goal achiever. Use this as your affirmation: **I am a goal achiever.**

Part of the problem many people have with goal setting is that they forget to check in with themselves to see how they're doing. It's a very good practice to evaluate your success at achieving your goals on a regular basis. You should check in monthly, quarterly, or at least every six months, and certainly annually.

I use the following categories of achievement or non-achievement for myself. Don't be afraid of non-achievement or not meeting your own goals. You only answer to yourself and you're not super human! Some people are hesitant to set goals just because of the fear of not achieving them. You're the only one who's going to know, so why not give it a try? Okay, here are the categories for achievement or not:

1. Doing okay
2. Doing better
3. Done
4. No longer needed or wanted
5. Doing worse
6. Needs lots of work
7. Failing. If so, then it's time to analyze if you really want this goal, and if you need this action item.

That's it. Now you can say, "I know how to set and achieve goals."

MOST COMMON MISTAKE: Thinking you don't have to write your goals down. I was skeptical, too, but the first time I ever wrote my goals down, I made it around the world. It works.

The action guide has the outline for you just discussed. I suggest you stop reading right now and work through your dream and goals. You'll see there are places for you to write down your dreams. But there's more space dedicated to the goals because that's how you get to your dreams faster, by turning your dreams into goals.

Remember: From entrepreneur to CEO, you want to know your goals and what you have to do to achieve them.

CHAPTER 4

No Risk, No Reward

Now we're getting into the fun stuff: **taking risks.** No Risk, No Reward. We've all heard that before. When faced with a risk, do you take the risk and seek the reward? Or does the risk scare you away? All great achievements require some sort of uncertainty, and therefore risk. More than likely, you'll have to let go of something in order to achieve your biggest goals.

Let's look at a few examples: If you want to be the top salesperson in your company, chances are you'll have to give up some evenings at home in favor of the office. If you want to start a coffee shop that's open on weekends, it's a good bet you'll no longer be attending your children's Saturday soccer games.

In the end, you get to decide what you're willing to sacrifice for your goals. Andre Gide said, "Man cannot discover new oceans unless he has the courage to lose sight of the shore." In other words, you can't run to second base unless you take your foot off of first. You're most likely going to have to take a risk in order to be a leader and to succeed as an entrepreneur.

Do you know what the number one obstacle is to achieving your greatest dreams? It's not money, it's not time, and it's not anything that you don't have. It's what you DO HAVE.

It's the good things in our lives that get in the way of great things.

Even in the best of economic times, the trappings of success will tempt us to set aside our dreams in favor of the security we already enjoy. Perhaps you would like to move abroad for a year to write, but your life here is good, comfortable, secure, and you can't see leaving it all behind. You have children, cars, a house, a job, club memberships, and responsibilities that keep you evenly happy. There's golf on Saturdays, yoga Thursday evenings, and the kids' soccer tournaments. Are these good aspects of your life bursting the bubble of your dreams? If you can't see giving up some of those things (you might want to keep the kids for example), you might not experience living high on top of a hill in an Italian villa writing the great novel. You get to decide.

Perhaps some people are used to taking risks more than others. I took a big risk to start our company, World Class Incentives. I had been working for another company for five years and when that situation became intolerable, I had no choice but to leave. I took a huge risk going out on my own. But there's something to taking a risk and putting everything on the line. You're almost forced to succeed. Certainly, there's more pressure to succeed. You have a mortgage to pay so you get up and you go to work and you focus. You make success happen.

After 20 years in business, I decided to take an even bigger risk. This one was for my personal passion. I had been dreaming of sailing around the world my entire life. I simply had to try to sail around the world. I just had to. The odds were certainly against my success. Only about 60 people a year *worldwide* succeed in completing a circumnavigation. The experience was like being on a runaway freight train careening down the tracks at high speed and I couldn't stop my momentum toward this goal. It was a wonderful feeling to want something so badly. And you as an entrepreneurial thinker will be blinded by your desire for success.

For a moment, think about what I left behind and what I risked to make my dream come true. I left my 20-year **career** and the day I sailed out the Golden Gate I basically committed career suicide. I was gone so long (six years) that my clients had moved on, become consultants on their own, or were no longer in a buying position. To go back into the events and incentive travel industry would have meant starting all over again.

I left my **income**. I had a pretty good middle-class income when I left. In a day, it went to zero. You want to talk about scary?

I left my **security**. By security, I mean everything from having a car in your driveway to the local grocer knowing your name. It's those familiar things, people, and events we surround ourselves with that make up our security. I left it all behind for adventure.

I left not only my physical **home**, but also my friends and family. I didn't know when or if I would ever see any of them again. I was so focused on going that I never considered the plan for return. Now I'm not suggesting you do that, as it was a very big risk and very scary. I tell you this to demonstrate that I was aware of the risk, and I was willing to take it.

Probably the most difficult of all was that I left my **identity**. I let go of who I was, who I had become, who I had built myself to be as an executive in the fast-paced world servicing Silicon Valley and other high profile companies in a wide variety of industries. I had built our company's reputation of being the best in the business and I let go of it all. I had no choice. These were the things I had to leave behind to fulfill my dream.

Is your current professional identity preventing you from exploring your emotional ambition? Let me repeat that. Is your professional identity and career track, or your social status, preventing you from exploring and achieving your emotional ambitions, which may include starting and running your own company?

What's in your way? Are you worried about who will watch the dog while you travel? You laugh, but many people let even the smallest things dissuade them from achieving great things. Logistics get in the way and dreams are set aside. Are you willing to LET GO of whatever it is that's holding you back?

I worked in an industry I loved, and was surrounded by wonderful peers and mutual respect. I had, over 20 years, built a good solid reputation for our company and myself. It was a great life and had every promise of continuing, but it had no promise of fulfilling my ultimate dream of sailing around the world. So I had to decide. Was it easy to walk away from this? Oh nooooo. No way. It was, in fact, extraordinarily difficult to do. But I had decided I wanted to live out my dream of sailing around the world and that meant giving up my career, income, security, home, and identity.

I'm not saying or even suggesting that you have to give up these elements in your life, but chances are you're going to have to give up something if you see yourself as an entrepreneur. All entrepreneurs have to take some sort of a risk to succeed. And because all leaders are risk takers, that means entrepreneurs must be leaders. So now you know why I'm so intent on teaching leadership skills.

Once you decide you're going to take a risk, then remind yourself you have decided. You're going to do this. Don't go back, don't shy away, and don't look again at the decision tomorrow unless new information appears.

So take a chance. Take a risk. It was Dale Carnegie who said, "Take a chance! All life is a chance. The person who goes farthest is generally the one who is willing to do and dare. The 'sure thing' boat never gets far from shore."

MOST COMMON MISTAKE: Trying to hang onto something that keeps us in our comfort zone, instead of letting go and being willing to break out and experience something new.

While I can't tell you to take a risk, I can show you how to evaluate your own willingness to take a risk.

Action Guide

For each goal you have, write down a risk you'll have to take in order to pursue the action steps you have listed. Identify any risks as you see them. They can be very simple. For example: If you want to open that bakery, the risk would be missing your kids' Saturday morning soccer games.

Now ask yourself, "Am I willing to take that risk?" Write down your answer. Committing your answer to paper can have a very powerful effect on your attitude about the risk when it's staring you in the eye. If you said you were willing to take the risk and you put it on paper, it's going to be easier to do.

Remember: Entrepreneurs, from small time operators to CEOs, know they have to take risks.

CHAPTER 5

How to Make Big Decisions by Setting Priorities

In this chapter, you're going to learn my method of how to make big decisions. You're also going to learn how to stay focused once you make those decisions. Do you have difficulty making decisions sometimes? I certainly do. Everybody faces decision-making challenges every day. You see a green light turn yellow—do you stop or run it? You choose between vine ripe tomatoes and cherry tomatoes, between olive oil from Spain or from Italy, the cheap car wash or the works. *Should I buy those new shoes? They would look so good on me but they're expensive … gee, I don't know.* Sometimes you choose to buy the shoes, and sometimes you don't. And sometimes, you don't choose. *Ehhh, never mind, I'll think about it.* Guess what, by making NO decision, you just made a decision not to buy the shoes.

The most common questions I'm asked are about two decisions I made in my life. The first decision was about leaving my job to start my own company. How did I do it? How did I decide? The second, and even more popular question is, how did I make the enormous decision to take the ultimate risk and leave everything behind to sail around the world. I'm not asked about money, time, or skills, but how. HOW did I make those decisions? And the answer to both is in one word: PRIORITIES.

You will start to get results right away by **making decisions based on your priorities.** "But Larry, wait, I don't know my priorities," you say. You don't? Okay, let's set your priorities.

Here's how I do it. I use the same system in my everyday life that we used on the boat. We had a system with a very sophisticated, complicated name. Are you ready for the complicated name? Okay, here it is: It's called "Priorities A–D" and it's your new best friend.

The main use of the system was to decide if we were ready to leave the marina or anchorage to go to sea. Were we ready to leave the dock, and head out across a bay, a channel, or a 3,000-mile ocean? Let me give you a simple example of priorities: If you're going to drive to Grandma's house a 100 miles away, and there are no gas stations between your house and hers, or in her town, then what do you need before you leave? The answer is simple: enough gas for 200 miles of travel. That would be an "A" on the scale. So, it went like this onboard the sailing vessel JULIA:

A = Must have before going to sea
B = Should have before going to sea
C = Would be nice to have before going to sea
D = Doubtful, but hopefully someday we'll get to that

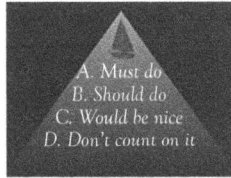

For example, having a working engine was an "A" or we couldn't even leave the marina. Varnishing the woodwork usually ended up in the "D" category because nobody really liked to do that and it wasn't a critical priority. There were enough A's, B's, and C's to keep us busy.

Now take this easy system and incorporate it into your entrepreneurial life and determine what your priorities are in your business. If you consistently make your decisions and choices based on them, the decision-making process will be much easier. Let your priorities serve as your guide and you'll be a more consistent leader of yourself and others.

What are your priorities as a leader and as an entrepreneur? Are they to help people? To teach others? To make money? To help others and make money? Which one is the A and which one is the B? Decide. Because when you have your priorities in place, every decision you make will become nearly automatic.

To leave my secure life and go sailing around the world, I made a few decisions based on my priorities. For example:

1. I chose to follow my passion and ignore my fears because my passion was my priority.

2. I chose adventure over security because adventure was the priority.

3. I chose experiences over saving money for the future because the experiences were my priority. In hindsight, that was an expensive priority! But while it left me with little money, I'm the richest person I know because of my experiences. And I would do it all over again.

When you have your priorities in place, decisions about everything become easier so why not include your personal life in your priorities? Anticipate what those priorities mean and their potential consequences. For example, if your "A" priority is to build a business at all costs, then you might run into some trouble with your home life. And if your "A" priority is to be a better golfer, that might impact your regular work life!

When you make decisions according to this system, you'll have much less stress because you know, at the very least, you're making the decision consistent with your priorities. You've already decided on them by doing your homework. Even if it ends up being wrong, there was a basis for making that decision.

Your decisions come after you have no more information one way or the other to help you decide. You have collected all of the information; you've rolled it around in your head; you've made pro and con lists; you've checked in with anybody you think can help; **you've considered your priorities;** and then you decide. Sometimes you think you don't have enough information, but you have to decide anyway.

When I decided to go sailing, I didn't I think I had enough information—and I was right—I didn't. I was unprepared to go sailing around the world. I didn't have the experience or the knowledge and I was scared, but I ignored my cold feet and went anyway. It was time to choose: stay in the default, or go sailing? I used my priorities to guide me and my "A" priority at the time was to sail around the world. I couldn't do that and still stay in business. That's how I made such a big decision.

Here's another example of decision making without enough information. When we were sailing in the Gulf of Aden, on our way to Oman, we were in serious pirate territory. One afternoon, we received a radio call from a man named Mohammed who said he could see us on radar and asked us to change our course 30 degrees so that we would avoid his 20-mile long fishing nets. Nets that long are not uncommon, but getting a call from someone who was concerned not only about his net, but also concerned about us getting caught in it, and for our well-being … well, in that pirate-laden part of the world, quite frankly seemed suspicious at the time.

I asked Mohammed some questions I thought only the captain of a fishing boat might know the answers to, and I then asked my crew who were all ears at the radio station because we were all on edge, what they thought. Was Mohammed telling the truth? Or was he steering us into a pirate trap? We didn't have any more information so all I had to go on was my feelings, my gut, and my trust—or not—in people.

Against the advice of some of my crew, I altered our course.

An hour later, we got another call from Mohammed thanking us for changing our course, that we were now safe from his net, and that he just wanted to remind us, "We're not all bad guys out here." I had to make that decision without all of the information I really needed, but I made it and stuck to it. When you make a decision, you do the best you can with the information you have, and then stick with it unless you get new information.

Basing decisions on your priorities will also keep you focused on the decision you made. Many people ask how I stayed focused on one thing for six years: sailing around the world. That was easy because my priority was to sail around the world. It was the "A" on my list and so everything else was on the list to serve the "A." Therefore, even though sailing around the world was the most difficult achievement in my life, it was also the easiest. I had one goal to focus on, getting my boat around the world. **My priorities kept me focused.**

In my business, our top priority was to deliver a **unique** and **flawless** group travel event for our corporate clients. Notice the two key elements in that priority mission statement. Our priority of uniqueness drove us to be creative and come up with events nobody had ever done in our industry. And we delivered these creative events flawlessly. Every decision we made was toward those two priorities. Because our customer service was so good, we turned our clients into raving fans.

As an entrepreneur, you must get comfortable making decisions by yourself. When you make a big decision, you expect there to be some sort of a fanfare, a marching band, trumpets should be blaring! "Hey, look at me, I made this big decision all by myself!" But it doesn't work that way. No matter how long we wait, that marching band never seems to show up. So ask yourself: Are you stalling on a decision because you're still waiting for your marching band? And remember, making **no decision IS making a decision**. When you make a big decision, it is often just the first step. The next step is to take action because it won't act on itself.

Decisions are often left unmade because of the fear of making the wrong choice. What if you make the wrong decision? First of all, it's not a "what if" question, but rather a "when" question? It's like running aground in your boat while sailing around the world. It's simply a matter of when.

You **will** eventually make a wrong decision even if you stick to your priorities. You're bound to make a wrong decision now and then. So? "But, but, but … what if it costs me money, or a client, or …?" It will. So what?

That may be the bad part of making a wrong decision. However, the good part outweighs the bad. Most likely, you won't make that same wrong decision twice. Learn from it, absorb what it teaches you, and insert it into your file bank. And then know that in the future, you'll be that much smarter. It's called experience.

Leadership is the ability to stay focused, and your priorities will keep you focused. Entrepreneurial Leaders know their priorities and use them to make decisions. Your priorities make you a decision-maker.

MOST COMMON MISTAKE: Not making a decision and fooling yourself into thinking that you actually decided something.

Action Guide

Go back to your goals and set priorities next to them. Now it's not just a gold star, it's A–D. Your priorities will guide you in so many decisions, so take your time and think about them.

The next exercise is to practice making decisions. Here's how to practice making decisions and demonstrate to yourself that you are a decisive person.

Write down three things you have been considering, contemplating, that you want to do or not do. I don't care what they are, big or small. It could be what you're going to prepare for lunch. Now DECIDE on those three things. I mean NOW. Right Now. There! Done! You're decisive. Once you've made the decisions, tell yourself that you're decisive. Look at you: you made a decision.

Do this three days in a row.

Practice sticking to your decisions. It will make you a more decisive person and you'll learn to trust in your decisions.

CHAPTER 6

Change Is Here to Stay

In this chapter, we're going to explore one of the most difficult aspects of leadership, especially for entrepreneurs: **CHANGE**. Not many people like change. Do you ever wish that things could just stay the same? You have your business, it's doing fine, and then along comes something that changes everything. A simple example is, say you're an oil company and then all of a sudden (or not all of a sudden, you just didn't notice it), solar panels and wind turbines are popping up everywhere threatening your oil company profits. You can struggle to hang on and push your product as the only solution, or you can jump into the development of solar and wind energy. For a big oil company, that's a slow change they have to accept. But as an entrepreneur you can react much more quickly.

Nearly all of us fear change. It's normal. We like constant, steady, reliable lives and that includes our business. Sorry, though. The one thing that you can count on that will never change in business is—are you ready?—there will always be change. Yes, I'm afraid so. But don't worry, because if you're not comfortable with change, you will be after this chapter. Knowing that change is the only constant in business (and in life, for that matter) is the first step to getting comfortable with it. Again, your business is much like a boat. It can only be steered if it's moving. Water has to be moving past the rudder in order for it to work. Even turning the steering wheel in your car doesn't work unless you're moving. So get used to it. Stagnation doesn't work. Therefore, movement is good and change is a good thing.

Let's start with changing our attitude about change. First of all, expect there will always be change. Maybe if you live in a cave, you can prevent it, but something tells me that if you're reading this and interested in Entrepreneurship, you're no sooner going to live in a cave than I am, which is not going to happen because there are no espresso machines in caves!

Now that you know there will always be change, you're not going to be surprised when it happens. You'll be able to deal with it in a calm productive manner. You know, something like, "Aahhh!!!" But at least you'll be able to catch yourself before going postal by saying, "Wait a minute, Larry said there would always be change, and here it is."

There are two kinds of change you'll experience as an entrepreneur. The first is "Proactive." That's when you know or suspect that something needs to be changed, or is going to change, and you initiate the minor revolution that's needed to deal with it.

Imagine you've been out sailing all day and you decide to drop your anchor for the night. You anchor in a beautiful bay with the wind blowing in the perfect offshore direction, and you know you're safe for the night. But then something starts gnawing at you. You see other boats leaving the bay. You look at the weather forecast and see a wind shift coming. If you don't leave this bay, the next thing you know, you'll be facing a lee shore with the wind blowing you dangerously close to the rocks. You proactively decide to move to the other side of the bay and sure enough, that's where you find all of the other boats that made the same proactive decision.

Let's take another example using sailing because it's such a good metaphor for business. First of all, who doesn't like sailing? Okay, never mind, I **do** know some people who don't like it, but it's so pretty, and soft, and gentle … Okay, never mind, I've seen some horrendous storms. Well, just go with me here.

Let's say we're sailing along on a particular course from San Francisco to the south/southwest and we notice that if we stay on this course, the current is going to push us off our route far enough to the north that we will miss the island of Tahiti. And that's bad because we want a beer! What do we do? We turn our steering wheel, change our course, and point a little further south so that the current will push us just north enough to keep us on a route for Tahiti. And in no time, say about three weeks, we're anchored, sitting on deck, and enjoying a beer because we were proactive in our change. If we hadn't been proactive, we would have missed the island and had to react by turning around and sailing back to Tahiti.

Be proactive in making changes by watching your industry. Learn to keep up with it. Read the trade magazines and online blogs. Look for trends, shifts, and changes. If your business is helping Moms, then read the Mommy blogs and listen to what they're saying. What are their needs, their complaints, and what are they talking about? You get the idea.

The second kind of change is Reactive change. Reactive change is often necessary in business if you don't see something coming and get blindsided. It's easy to do and it's often caused by circumstances beyond your control. If you were watching really closely, you might have seen it coming, but I recognize that you can't be so busy watching an industry that you avoid running your business! Then you would just be an "industry watcher" and that by itself is a full-time job.

Let's use the same anchoring example we just talked about. Suppose you don't notice the other boats leaving the anchorage, and you don't look at the forecast so you don't know there's a wind shift coming. You fall asleep to the gentle breeze, the soft rolling of the boat, and then at midnight, (it always happens at midnight), BAM! The wind direction changes 180 degrees and you are now dangerously close to the lee shore and rocks. What do you do? You **react** by hauling up your anchor and moving to the other side of the bay or you head out to sea, but you don't just sit there waiting for circumstances to blow you onto the beach. You have reacted.

Which is better? Proactive or Reactive? Surely proactive is, but hey, we're not all that perfect. The anchoring examples I'm using are real. I've been proactive, and I've had to be reactive because I wasn't paying close enough attention to the situation. When anchoring, you not only must take into account what the conditions are, but also what they could become. It's a lot to think about. As an entrepreneur you don't have a big team of marketing people telling you industry trends, so you have to be even more vigilant and aware of what's going on around you.

I've made good and bad decisions in sailing and in business. As I said, the anchoring examples are real and I've been forced to weigh anchor in the middle of the night in a very reactive way. In business, I have been proactive, and I've been reactive, forced by circumstances that were beyond my control.

As I mentioned, my business was in the incentive travel industry—our job was to take the top salespeople, dealers, distributors, and other important VIPs of a company on the most extraordinary trips that money could buy. About 95 percent of our business was international.

We took groups to London, Rome, Paris, Vienna, Bangkok, Singapore, Hong Kong, Rio, and the list goes on and on. Our clients, leaders in their industry, wanted the best of the best, and the most exciting trips possible, so we searched to the far ends of the globe to create these events. We were doing great, really on a roll, and then, in 1990, Iraq invaded Kuwait and international travel stopped like a freight train running into a mountain. Without exception, all of our international travel stopped. Clients can-celled trips, paid the cancellation fees to the hotels, and told us they might consider moving their event to Phoenix, or Hawaii, but most of the trips were just cancelled or postponed for another time. We were told, "Maybe next year or the year after when it's safe for Americans to travel."

We had to react fast. We knew our clients still had the budget to spend because those dollars were already allocated to the program. We couldn't get them to travel, and we couldn't very well make a profit on marking up cash. Who wants to pay $1.15 for $1? So we shifted gears and became a leading supplier of merchandise award catalog programs. You've seen these incentive catalogs. You know, where instead of winning a trip to Switzerland, you win a million points in a catalog and you can refur-nish your house, get bikes for the kids, a new TV, new kitchen appliances, and all of the other "safe, stay at home" items you want. The country was cocooning and we jumped on it. We approached our clients and many of them agreed it was a good idea. Instead of going out of business like many of our competitors, we survived the slow period until travel came back. We succeeded while other travel companies failed because we recognized that change was happening and we reacted just in time.

You too can act quickly in Proaction (yes, I invented a new word) or Reaction. Being an entrepreneur means you don't have to run every decision by others or through a committee. Or, if you do, it's a very small committee, such as mine, which consists of three: Me, Myself, and I.

On the down side, you don't get to run decisions by others. So don't delay, act quickly. Sure, do some investigating as to what's happening with the change you're seeing, and ask those who might advise you well, but make a timely decision. In other words, **act fast because you can!**

Recognize that change is going to happen and that it's Okay. Think of the good things about change. While sailing around the world, if we didn't like our anchorage, we could change it. If we didn't like our course, we could change it. If we didn't like the country we were in, we could change it. **The ability to accept and recognize the positive aspects of change is the sign of a true leader.** Remember you're supposed to be enjoying your entrepreneurial life, so enjoy the changes and get used to them. Wouldn't life be boring if it was the same every day?

Remember the cool thing about expecting change in business. It all changes continually anyway. So, in the end, you're expecting what is going to happen. That's being a leader!

MOST COMMON MISTAKE: Expecting there will be no change in your daily business and that you can just "get to that point" of ease and not having to think proactively.

Action Guide

Proactively change something very small in your life today. Change your drink, change something you eat, or change something you wear. Change your blouse, your shirt, your socks, I don't care, just change something and recognize that you proactively did it.

The next exercise is going to take some more awareness on your part. I want you to react to something that changes and be okay with it. No kidding. Friends are scheduled to come over for a BBQ, and at the last minute they call to say they can't make it. What's your first reaction? Uh-huh, anger. I thought so. Mine would be the same. But now consciously, change that reaction to one of okay. BBQ the same food, put the extras away, and have dinner already done for tomorrow. You reacted to change and it was okay.

It's these small events and your reactions that will give you the practice and strength to handle the big changes when they come along. Why the BBQ exercise? Because it just happened to me the other day and I caught myself having a bad reaction … and I know better. So join me in a salute to BBQ'ing for yourself. And throw another shrimp on the barbie!

CHAPTER 7

Using Fear to Your Advantage

And now my favorite topic: FEAR. Really, Larry? Your favorite topic is fear? Are you feeling okay? Yes, I am. The reason fear is my favorite topic is that I was able to figure out how to manage it. And now I get to share that with you. Are you experiencing any fear about being an entrepreneur? Of course you are, every entrepreneur experiences fear, or they're very good about covering it up. It's part of the entrepreneurial deal. Fear is part of the package. However, this is a good day for you, because right here you're going to learn to manage your fears. Right Now.

We've all heard a kid say, "You're not the boss of me!" It's funny when they say it because while they may be telling you to leave them alone and let them make their own decisions, what they're saying with that statement is, "No thing and no body tells me what to do or how to do it." Often, kids don't have fears so they don't have to re-train themselves … yet. Most of you, including me, have lived enough years to let some fears establish themselves inside of our heads. So pretty much, what we're going to say to your fears is, "You're not the boss of me." Don't worry, because I'm going to show you how.

First, what is fear? **False Expectations Appearing Real**. Mark Twain said, "I've had a lot of worries in my life, most of which never happened."

I want to acknowledge there are more ways to address your fears than just what I'm telling you. Others have said to:

- Overcome your fears.
- Master your fears.
- Face your fears; stare them down and defeat them.
- Do the thing you fear most and you'll no longer have that fear.
- Avoid the things you fear.

I recognize there are multiple ways to manage fears, but I respectfully disagree with these solutions. I'm sharing **my** boardroom and ocean-tested method. I know it works facing 30-foot seas, staring down Komodo dragons, and calling CFOs of billion dollar companies asking why our payment isn't on time. It works swimming with sharks and sea snakes, too.

Those are just some of my experiences that scared me. I know you have fears too. Big fears. What are they? Have you just had a newborn and are wondering how you'll pay for their college education with your entrepreneurial startup? Are you searching for a job? Have you just been promoted and don't really feel qualified? Have you just started a new business on your own? Do you have "The jitters?" Your fears are valid and don't let anybody tell you, "Oh, don't be afraid of that." If you're afraid, you're afraid. I will show you how to manage that fear.

If I were to ask you what the scariest moment in your life was, could you tell me? The riskiest? The most thrilling? Take a moment to picture them in your mind. For many, I happen to know the answer was learning to ride a bicycle. Can you imagine that the scariest moment of one's life was learning to ride a bike? And even if this was the scariest moment in your life, that is what I call False Expectations Appearing Real.

If you were to ask me those same questions above, the answer might be dodging pirates in the Gulf of Aden, being chased by Komodo Dragons in Indonesia, or battling the worst storm of our lives in the middle of the Red Sea. My two-man crew and I had been caught in the exact wrong place at the wrong time in the Red Sea. It was a storm that came 24 hours early and its strength was way underestimated. Imagine our small boat flying off the top of a 30-foot wave and slamming down into the trough below, shaking and shuddering like a cannon. The seas were not only huge, but they were steep, and they were coming fast. I remember counting: one thousand one, one thousand two, one thousand three, and BAM! Another one would hit us. The winds had built the seas up to this huge state by blowing over 55 knots for more than 24 hours, stronger than a full gale, a near hurricane. The noise was relentless. The wind sounded like a wounded animal as it howled through the rigging. It was exhausting.

And we were exhausted. We had been up for more than 24 hours and I was hallucinating. I was seeing images and shapes of walls and mountains in front of us. And I was hearing voices in my head, more voices than I usually hear! We were alone. There were no other boats out there, and there's no Egyptian or Saudi Arabian coast guard you can call for help or advice.

All I really wanted to do was go down below, crawl into a bunk, pull the covers up over my eyes, and wish it all away.

But then I looked at my crew, Ken and CJ and saw their eyes were as wide as saucers. They were really scared. What about me, was I scared? I wouldn't use that word, as I think terrified is more appropriate! You'd have to be crazy not to be scared in those conditions. The fear was definitely founded; I was afraid for myself, the boat, and most of all, for my crew.

But Fear—like most emotions—is contagious. I was captain and I was the leader, and the last thing I needed was a crew frozen with fear. I needed my crew to do their jobs for the overall safety of the boat. I needed to inspire confidence, motivation, and passion and it didn't matter how rough it was. I didn't have any choice but to lead. If I was terrified, how did I get through my fears right then?

We all know that fear causes one of two reactions: fight or flight. So I checked to see if there were any flights going out of the middle of the Red Sea that morning (Okay, not really but it crossed my mind!). Our only choice was to stay and fight, and to learn about fear. I learned a lot about fear that day. I learned that

> *Fear is: Nature's way of making us focus on the task at hand. It sharpens your senses, and makes you more alert. You can use your fears to your advantage.*

Do you remember that "on your toes" feeling from your scary moment? Most likely it was caused by fear. I used to call it the "Jitters" on purpose so I could avoid telling myself I was afraid. Now I use fear to my advantage and I'm going to show you how to do just that.

There are only two steps to learning to use fear to your advantage.

1. The first step is to recognize that it's there. You've felt and seen fear. If you had been with us that day in the Red Sea, you would have seen my palms sweating, my eyes bright and darting all around, my

muscles all pumped up, and you could have heard my heart beating through my chest from three feet away. Think back to your scary moment and you'll remember the same signs. When you recognize the fear, you also see that it's making you focus, it's making your senses sharper, and you're more alert. Believe me, when I was at the wheel in 30-foot seas, I was focused, sharp, and alert. And while I was still afraid, I was a better performer. I was 100 percent focused, sharp as a tack, and very alert!

2. The next step in using fear to your advantage is a little bit trickier. Accept that you're afraid. Yes, you must accept and **embrace** the fear. By taking this next step, you disarm the fear. You take away its power when you say this to yourself: "Okay, I'm afraid. Now, instead of letting it freeze me up, since I know the benefits fear can give me, I'm going to let it in." Then you can embrace being focused, sharp, and alert. You can, right there and then, use those new-found powers to your advantage. Fear is like that little red devil that sits on your shoulder and tells you to have that second cocktail, or third cookie. When you recognize and embrace the fear, it's like you're saying to your fears, "You can come along for the ride, but you no longer have any say in what I feel, or how I act. I know you're there and I know you're trying to do bad things, but I know better. Larry told me that you could do good things for me! So there! YOU'RE NOT THE BOSS OF ME!" Don't listen to the wind as it howls through the rigging trying to scare you. Get behind the wheel and start steering.

It was fear of going out of business when the Gulf War broke out that forced us to re-think our business model of incentive travel. Being afraid of losing the business is what drove the search for other incentives such as the merchandise catalog.

Fear has amazing power for you when you harness it.

If you think I'm one of those people who are fearless, think again.

I remember scuba diving near the island of Niue, an island nation in the South Pacific Ocean commonly known as the Rock of Polynesia. Niue is 1,500 miles northeast of New Zealand. One of its biggest appeals is the incredibly clear water. Because the island is mostly limestone, there isn't much soil runoff so the waters remain crystal clear with 150-foot visibility. We stopped in Niue on our way across the pacific to scuba dive and see the world-renowned clear water.

Much to my chagrin, Niue also has a significant poisonous sea snake population. When it comes to snakes, I'm not keen on even the gentle garden variety, let alone these serpents. Even so, I had to deal with rattlesnakes while working as a river rafting guide back in my youth. The rattlers would slither their way into camp and tuck into a warm spot near a rock, and invariably one of the guests would discover it and scream: "Aaaaaaaah! S…Sn…Sna…Snak…SNAKE!" We'd rig a long stick with a loop on the end, capture the angry snake, and carry it flailing and squirming down to the river knowing it would find a new home further downstream. I hated that job but couldn't very well show my fear—at least not outwardly. Now I'm older and admit my dislike of snakes. No. Dislike is too small a word. I freely admit I have a FEAR of snakes.

Sitting at anchor in Niue, we could see the sea snakes' heads break the surface long enough to breathe before heading down to the ocean floor where they prefer to shelter until needing more air. They're 2- to 4-feet long, an inch in diameter, and are quite pretty with silver and black stripes. Okay, they're not pretty; there's nothing really pretty about any snake in my mind, and these are so poisonous, one bite will kill you. They have small mouths, though, and it would be difficult for them to bite. Still, you wouldn't want to give them a chance.

The diving is so good in Niue, and the law is that you must dive with the local company, so there's a waiting list—and you go when you're called. The morning of our first dive, I asked the dive master where we were headed to which he casually replied, "Snake Gully." With a hint of desperation, I asked, "Isn't there any other place we can explore?" He replied with his smart New Zealand wit, "Sure is, mate, lots of places, but today is Tuesday, and we always dive Snake Gully on Tuesdays." (Groan)

For a moment, my thoughts raced: I could feign illness right now, I could break some of my equipment or I could come up with an earache in an instant. Yet, I chose to dive. I wasn't going to let a few hundred deadly poisonous snakes ruin my day. There were so many snakes that we had to watch out where we were swimming so we didn't bump into them.

Most were on the bottom in piles like a scene out of *Indiana Jones* (who also had a fear of snakes, so I don't feel so bad), and I got the shivers taking in the scene. At any given time, a dozen or so were swimming around us, up to or down from the surface and we had to push the water away in front to ensure not bumping into them. With my fear of snakes, this took all the bravery I could muster, but I recognized and embraced my fear and made it through with a feeling of exhilaration. However, I still have no desire to do that dive again.

Once back on the dive boat, we saw a pod of spinner dolphins and motored over to see how close we could get. We jumped into the clear warm water and swam slowly toward the dolphins, which were much friendlier than snakes, I might add. While most of them were not interested in a bunch of humans flailing about, two of the sleek mammals were so playful they kept swimming under and around us in circles and frolicking like young puppies—that is, if puppies weighed 200 pounds. This was a dream come true for me: We were actually swimming with dolphins in the wild!

Unbelievable. And it was something I never would have experienced had I given in to fear. I didn't avoid the fearful thing, I didn't overcome it, I'm still afraid of poisonous sea snakes. I faced the fear but I didn't defeat it. I just learned to accept and embrace it. And that just made it a nonissue.

If I could recognize and embrace those fears, then you can too. I don't have any special fear blockers or any other secrets on this subject. George Patton said: "There is a time to take counsel of your fears, and there is a time never to listen to any fear."

It's okay to be afraid because fear can be your ally. It can work to your advantage, especially if you anticipate the fear before it happens. Then you can examine the fear and see logically that it's probably filling you with false evidence that appears real. And always keep this in your back pocket: **passion trumps fear**.

As an entrepreneur, you should expect to be afraid sometimes. But now you know how to manage your fears.

Most Common Mistake: Believing something is scarier than it really is. Often, once you dive in and swim with the snakes, you discover it's not so bad.

Action Guide

Write down one thing you are afraid of.

Under that, write the three elements that make you afraid of that one thing.

Example of a fear:

Crossing the ocean.

Elements that make up this fear:

1. Losing sight of land
2. Big storms in the middle of the ocean
3. Running out of food

Next, provide the logical answer to those fears.

Example:

1. It is actually safer out at sea that near shore. A not-so-famous sailor named Jacobson once said, "It's not the ocean that gets you, it's the hard bits around the edges." Most boats get in trouble when they are close to land, not at sea.
2. Most of the time, you can see storms coming on satellite weather pictures. Preparation and training for impending storms helped me to manage my fears about them.
3. We can always fish for food—and we did. We caught lots of fish!

CHAPTER 8

You Don't Need to Know It All

What if you don't know what you're doing? The simple answer is: You don't have to be the expert to try something. You can become the expert along the way.

I am often asked about this very important point, "How can I be a successful leader, and/or how can I be a successful entrepreneur if I don't know what I'm doing?" People ask, "What if I don't know anything about business? I've never been the leader type. I barely know how to use a calculator. How can I run a business? How can I lead others?" Sound familiar?

The truth is, **you don't have to know what you're doing now. You just have to start.** I am the living proof of this. I was not prepared to sail around the world. I didn't have the knowledge or experience necessary to face the unexpected overwhelming challenges involved in sailing a boat all the way around the world. All I had was a boat and a dream but I went anyway. Based on my business experience, I already knew I didn't have to be the expert to try something—I figured I'd learn along the way—and I did.

Nor did I know much about business when I first stepped out to be an entrepreneur. I figured I'd learn along the way and I did.

If you don't believe me, let's look at others who didn't know what they were doing when they first started: Henry Ford, The Wright Brothers, Steve Jobs, Mark Zuckerberg, Thomas Edison … Do I need to keep going?

None of these people knew how to do what they were attempting—they just started. The classic example in modern history is of course Thomas Edison and the invention of the light bulb. The legend goes something like this: it supposedly took 1,000 tries before he found the material that worked as a light bulb filament. When asked how he felt about failing 999 times, he answered, "I didn't fail. I succeeded in finding 999 elements that wouldn't work."

Stop and think about that positive attitude. It's really quite amazing.

Let's take a look at some examples of what you might not know how to do.

1. Social media—If you don't know how to get the word out about your business or product or service, then hire a virtual assistant to do it for you. You can find them easily on the Internet. Leadership is recognizing what you don't know, and filling that gap with someone who does. Thus, you might hire a virtual assistant to get you started while you learn along the way.

2. Bookkeeping—Can you operate a calculator? Can you download an accounting software program? Then there's nothing you can't do in business bookkeeping. If you can't do your books, find a virtual assistant who can. I'm not allowing you any excuses here.

3. Computers—If you struggle with computers, then take lessons. Take lessons from a live person, or you can go to YouTube for free lessons on just about any software you can imagine.

4. Advertising and PR—Before I became savvy about promotion, I hired companies to do my PR for me. I knew enough to know what I didn't know. I hired companies that gave me great PR, and I hired companies that were a complete waste of money. I watched their successes and failures and learned lessons from them all. Now I know much more about PR and social media, but I still use an outside company so I'm free to create content.

5. Sourcing of products or materials—Say you want to sell baby clothes as your new business. Where do you find them? Have you looked on the Internet? You can find a supplier in minutes. There's an answer for every single one of you who is thinking about what you don't know how to do in business.

6. Leading others in your business—If you don't have much experience leading others in business, don't worry about that either. You're learning here as you go, and we're going to get specific in Chapter 11.

If what I'm saying isn't making you comfortable enough, there is a way to make you feel better about not knowing what you're doing. Make a plan. You've no doubt heard the saying, "Failure to plan is planning to fail" and it's true. However, planning too far ahead and worrying about not knowing how you'll handle things in the distant future is wasted effort on your part. Think short-term, as in the next few action items you need to take. Then add long-term thinking.

If you're still thinking: "But how can I make a plan if I don't know what I'm doing?" your plan can be simple. It can be as simple as wanting to sell imported shoes. It doesn't take a genius to figure out that if you want to sell imported shoes, you're going to need a supplier. Mexico? China? The questions that follow are logical: What kind of shoes? Men? Women? Children? Casual? Dress? Have you recognized your market as waterproof women's sailing shoes? Do a bit of research to discover if that's a viable market. Then find your supplier, get a price, double it, and that's your sales price. There, you have a plan and you can fill in the details as you go. You may think this is too simplistic but it's better than waiting and waiting to get everything ready and every question answered. If you wait for that, you'll never begin.

Remember, "Once you have a plan, THEN you have something to change."

MOST COMMON MISTAKE: Thinking something is harder than it is without actually giving it a try.

Action Guide

Do something new today that you don't already know how to do. It could be a new exercise in the gym. It could be looking for a virtual assistant online. You could try writing a short three-line poem. How about writing your company mission statement or re-writing it? Remember, there's no such thing as good writing, only good re-writing. You could try going to the store via a different route. Break out of your comfort zone. What if you walked or rode your bike to the store? Now you'd really be pushing the envelope!

NEXT: **Learn** something new. I don't care what it is. Your goal is to prove to yourself that you can learn something new. Learn how to use new software, cook something from a new recipe, read about a foreign country, and learn something you didn't know. That's it. Just know that you are not beyond learning. Half the battle in this chapter is simply giving yourself the confidence that you can do this.

CHAPTER 9

How to Stick With It, Even in Tough Times

Staying power, tenacity, perseverance, resolve, drive, you can choose your preferred word for "hanging in there." Results come from perseverance, not knowledge. Do I have to repeat the story about Thomas Edison? No, I think you get it. And it was Edison who said, "Genius is one percent inspiration and 99 percent perspiration." We all have inside of us an enormous potential for perseverance. There are countless stories of people surviving in life rafts, of persevering through horrible conditions, of people rising to the occasion and reaching heights beyond wherever they dreamed they could go.

That's because we all have the ability to dig deep inside of us for strength and tenacity when we need it in emergency. The difficult part is to find that strength and tenacity in your everyday life.

I once stayed at the helm of our boat for nearly 36 hours straight with just a few short sleep breaks. I did that because I had to. You too have done something that took an enormous of tenacity to complete. Think back about that. Was it late night studying, training as an athlete, having the strength to care for your children, or something else? Whatever it was, ask yourself what drove you?

Survival is what drives perseverance in dangerous situations. Passion is what drives that same perseverance in non-dangerous situations.

Whether it's survival or passion, to truly be a leader and a success in business, you have to persevere, which means not letting anyone or anything stand in the way of your goals, objectives, and dreams. To make it around the world, for six years we had to overcome and persevere through an enormous amount of challenges and my crew and I were tested every single day.

In the Red Sea, there was no way a full-blown gale of nearly 60-knot winds and 30-foot seas were going to stand in my way.

When we were in Indonesia, on the island of Rinca, we had been at Komodo National Park because I was always fascinated with Komodo Dragons. For lack of a better description, these are giant poisonous lizards, and when I say giant, I mean 12 feet long and about 4 feet around! They lumber slowly with their clawed feet and yellow forked-tongue as they hunt their prey such as water buffalo or horses. They hunt in packs and if you're unlucky enough to be cornered by them, you're a goner. Their method of killing is to bite you just once so their poison enters your system. They'll then follow you around for days until your nervous system collapses and then they'll eat you while you're still alive.

After viewing these giant reptiles under the supervision of a national park guide, my first mate Ken and I were left to fend for ourselves and we headed back along a narrow trail toward the bay where our boat was anchored. We were in shorts and sandals casually sauntering along when we looked ahead and saw two giant Komodo Dragons coming toward us on the three-foot wide trail. To our right was a 70-degree inclined steep cliff. To our left was a gorge about a hundred feet deep. Our only choice was to turn around and run! We ran as fast as our sea legs in sandals could carry us along the trail back toward the Park Headquarters, but we were no match for the Dragons. They may look slow, but they started chasing us and we found out the hard way that they can run at 15 miles an hour! They were gaining on us fast, so we were down to only two choices: up the cliff or jump into the gorge. That narrowed it down to one choice. We scrambled, climbed, clawed, pulled, and otherwise inched ourselves up this steep cliff grabbing clumps of grass, a tree branch here and there, a protruding rock, you name it, anything. With our hands dug into the cliff, and scared out of our wits, we pulled ourselves up to about 15 feet above the trail. We didn't know if dragons could climb but we had gone as high as we could go and so we just held on there. As the dragons arrived on the trail under us, they stopped. One had what looked like half a chicken hanging out of its mouth and we figured they were eyeing us as dessert. "Hang on!" we kept telling each other. For what seemed like the longest minute in history, the dragons hung out at the bottom of the trail looking up at us as if to say, "And stay off of our trail!" Then they casually moved along. When they were well out of sight, we slid down the cliff and sprinted with all our might toward the bay, jumped in our dinghy, and sped back to the safe haven of our boat at anchor. That time, the perseverance only had to last a minute, but the fear factor made it seem like an hour. This was a case of survival—we had no choice other than hanging on—unless we wanted to be eaten!

There were plenty more fearful events that required perseverance on my journey around the world. For example, we dodged pirates sailing through "pirate alley" in the Gulf of Aden and these were not Disney pirates. Johnny Depp was nowhere to be found. We were afraid for three full days on that passage.

We nearly lost our mast in a storm on our way to Australia because we lost the forestay, the half-inch thick wire that runs from the top of the mast to the bow of the boat. In 15-foot seas, 45-knot winds, and pouring rain that came sideways in sheets, we were forced to crawl our way to the foredeck and rig a temporary forestay to save the mast. It was physically and mentally taxing and an extremely difficult enterprise, but our survival depended on succeeding. That same day, we lost our autopilot and ended up hand steering 550 miles the rest of the way to Australia. To this day, I still get the shivers when I tell this story. We persevered.

We missed being wiped out by the tsunami in Thailand by the skin of our teeth … simply because of a whim, an impulse purchase of airline tickets to come back to the States for Christmas. Otherwise, our boat and we would have been destroyed while anchored at Patong Beach when the first wave hit. Instead, we were in San Francisco, and our boat was hauled out into a boat yard having work done on it.

When we returned to a Thailand filled with devastation, it was a real test of our will to persevere and continue sailing around the world. The death and mayhem were incredibly depressing, and our morale sunk to the lowest of the journey making me question my ability to continue. To be candid, I was plain old-fashioned afraid of continuing and of what would happen to us next. Then I heard my mother's voice in the back of my head reminding me, "You don't finish some of the time. You finish all of the time—no matter what."

I nearly drowned in a scuba diving accident at the bottom of the Red Sea. I was diving alone—absolutely forbidden in diving—and I got tangled in an anchor line I was trying to free. I was running out of air and only at the last minute, when I used my knife to cut my way out of the tangled mess did I make it to the surface with zero air left in my tank. I lived because of my perseverance.

We lost our autopilot multiple times, had to rebuild our engine, had more mechanical failures than I can recall, and had emotional breakdowns too. We faced and overcame challenges each and every day for six years. That's a long time and it took an enormous amount of effort to persevere.

We all have a huge amount of strength, tenacity, and perseverance inside of us. It shows up in emergencies when we're faced with lions, tigers, and bears ... and dragons and huge waves. You can access that strength before you need it but you have to dig deeper.

The skill here is in developing tenacity and perseverance. They are learned traits that come from practice.

It's easy to persevere under good conditions. Anybody can do that. That's not tenacity, that's just going with the flow. To persevere through tough times, it helps to have had practice. You also must recognize when you're in a situation that requires perseverance. When you see that you're going to be in it for the long haul or you recognize the survival situation you're in, that makes it real. Once you recognize how real it is, you can find the subconscious drive to dig deep for the strength you need to get through that situation.

I came very close to turning around so many times along the way. It would have been so much easier to just throw in the towel but I knew I had to persevere. I also knew I had that strength inside of me. There was only one thing that could stop me, and that would be sailing back underneath the Golden Gate Bridge, and that's exactly what happened.

After six years, 40,000 nautical miles, and 40 countries, we sailed back underneath the Golden Gate Bridge and I made my big dream of sailing all the way around the world come true. This just proves that anybody can make his or her dream come true! If I can do that, then surely you can achieve a higher level of leadership and entrepreneurial success.

Nobody died aboard the boat JULIA, nobody lost a limb, nobody was even seriously injured, and believe me there are 100 ways to die out there.

My circumnavigation is a story of good times, of surviving rough times, and emerging stronger for having been tested. And it's a story about perseverance.

If you want to succeed as a leader in business, you must persevere. You must embrace your goal of success with everything you've got. Be emotional, be passionate, be charged, and be strong enough to hang in there.

> *Work to persevere against all challenges that stand in your way. It's easy to persevere under good conditions, but you must persevere under all conditions.*

You might be wondering, "How do I work to persevere. What specifically can I do?" Here are some tools to help you dig deeper for your perseverance and tenacity:

First of all, having a positive attitude helps you persevere. You've heard this so many times from others and all they tell you is, "keep a positive attitude." Don't you get sick of it sometimes? "Have a positive attitude, have a positive attitude," and it makes you want to scream because sometimes keeping a positive attitude is hard to do.

> *Circumstances and events happen, often beyond our control. Because of our human nature, we try to control them, and much of our frustration comes from the fact that we cannot always control circumstances and events.*

We can still try to take as much control of our lives as possible and not be victims of these circumstances and events. I think you know me well enough by now to recognize that I believe in taking control of your own life! But you can't control if a tsunami hits your home. You can't control if a sudden storm comes up and throws 30-foot seas at you. Well, I could have controlled that by not going sailing in the first place and staying home with a good secure life. But you're an entrepreneur, and a good secure life without risk is probably not in your genes. Perhaps you've heard William Shedd's quote, "A ship is safe in harbor, but that's not what ships are for."

Can you think of something in your life, either personal or business that you couldn't control? Of course you can, but:

While you can't always control what happens, you can control how you react.

How you react IS YOUR ATTITUDE. How you react to situations, circumstances, and events is the only thing you can truly control. When you control how you react, you control your attitude. When you control your attitude, you control your feelings. You then have the sensation, rightfully so, that you are in control of your life. I don't mean that you should be calculated all of the time and not let any of your emotions drive you, because emotional response is also important. There's a time and place for emotion, and for control.

When we arrived in Australia after surviving a rough four-day storm in which we nearly lost our mast, our autopilot twice, and a few other major problems along the 11-day passage, a newspaper reporter said, "Wow, what a horrible passage you had. Have you ever had such a terrible time at sea?" I replied,

> "Horrible? Are you kidding? This was our best passage yet. We saved the boat, we learned to work together as a team, we learned to manage the boat in terrible weather, and we're here to talk about it. We rose to the occasion and we were at our best. It was a huge success. It's all how you look at it."

As a leader, it's important to keep a positive attitude. It's easy to see the bad in iffy circumstances. It takes more effort to see the good, but dig deeper and you'll find it. It's in there; you just have to look harder.

The next way to learn to persevere is to learn how to talk to yourself. As a writer of articles, books, and speeches, I talk to myself all the time. If you were to walk by my desk, you might think I was nuts. While that may be possible, it's usually just me giving myself Positive Self Talk. It's common neuroscience knowledge that when we speak to ourselves, we listen. Whatever we tell ourselves, we hear. And what we hear, we believe, especially if it's coming from a "reliable" source such as ourselves. We usually believe ourselves.

If that's the case, then tell yourself some good things! And tell others good things too. Start here with these four criteria about what you say to yourself:

Is It True?

You may tell yourself, "I'm not good with numbers." (Here's a secret, neither am I). So I add to what I say, "I'm not good at numbers ... so I need to practice working with numbers and get better at it." Or I'll say something like, "I know numbers aren't my strong suit but knowing people is. Therefore, I'm going to hire someone who IS good at numbers." Do you see the difference? If you're telling yourself something that is true but is negative, add something positive to it. Now imagine how this goes over when speaking to others you are leading. Perhaps a co-worker carries a beat-up briefcase that looks shoddy, and represents your company in a negative way. Instead of saying, "That's an ugly beat-up briefcase," try this: "Does that brief case have a history in your family? Sure looks like it's been through a lot. What do you say; we give it a rest, and go get you a new one of your choice? I'm buying." No negative self-talk. Got it?

Is It Beneficial?

Does it help me? How is it helping me? When doing a pose in yoga and holding it for a minute, which seems like an eternity, sometimes I can feel that I'm losing the proper shape of the pose. I could, and am sometimes tempted to say, "Larry, you're not very good at yoga." But that's not useful talk.

Instead, thanks to my wonderful yoga teacher, I have learned to say, "How great that you're holding on for a full minute. It doesn't matter how you look, you're holding on. Keep holding on." That's beneficial talk. This is not only important for you, but as a leader it's important to those you are leading to see your confidence. Is it beneficial? Is this going to help the person you are leading? Saying something to a co-worker like, "That was a lousy meeting you just ran," is only going to make them feel bad. What a different reaction you would get if you asked, "How do you feel the meeting went? Could it have gone better? Do you want help reviewing it so the next meeting is even better?"

See the difference? Degrading someone is not leadership. Helping them is.

Is It Important?

Sometimes self-talk is just blabbing on about nothing and you'll be amazed when you start analyzing what you're saying to yourself. What information are you telling yourself that has no importance? Listen to what you say to yourself.

We are so determined as leaders to be careful about what we say to others, it's easy to forget about watching what we say to ourselves.

If you were a coaching client of mine, I'd be asking what you said to yourself today. This week? This month? If I'm not going to coach you, then I trust you'll do this for yourself. It's incredibly powerful to focus on speaking to yourself about important things. And this doesn't just apply to you. When speaking to others, if you don't like the tie they're wearing, is it really important?

Is It Timely?

Is this the right time to be asking about this? Are there other things that might be more important right now? Back to "I'm not good with numbers." If you're just starting out a small home business, until you have a dollar come in the door, it really doesn't matter if you're good at numbers or not! It would be timelier to work on bringing that first dollar in the door.

As a leader, when interacting with others, give a thought to whether or not it's timely. Can it wait? Should it wait? Or perhaps now is the right time. Practice asking this of yourself and soon you'll be doing it automatically and subconsciously.

Remember that perseverance is a skill best learned from practice. You can practice by keeping a positive attitude, positive self-talk, and digging deep for the good in all circumstances and events.

MOST COMMON MISTAKE: Thinking you don't have the strength to achieve something—when you really do. You just haven't dug deep enough for it yet.

SECOND MOST COMMON MISTAKE: Underestimating the perseverance it will take to achieve a big goal you have set. Be realistic about how easy or hard something is going to be and prepare for it.

Action Guide

I'd like you to look back at your goals.

Looking at your goals, where will you need strength and perseverance? Prepare yourself for what and when you think will be difficult issues.

Look at your top three goals and underneath each one write down what type of strength you're going to need. Emotional, physical, new skill sets, practice of your art or presentation, patience, or someone else to do it for you?

Just like expecting fear and change—and planning for them—you can plan what strength you'll need to achieve a goal. Write it down. Contemplate the course, obstacles, and solutions ahead of time. Write them down. Did I mention that you should write them down?

CHAPTER 10

Live With Passion

The ninth key to being a successful entrepreneur is to live with passion. Its importance is underestimated and sometimes it is confusing as to what passion means. I like to break passion into two categories.

1. Passion for what you do.
2. Passion for how you do something.

Let's start with **passion for what you do**. Are you filled with joy, eagerness, and enthusiasm for what you do daily? How about for your entrepreneurial idea? Do you love it? Does it show to others? Passion means wanting something—how badly do you want it? Do you walk with slumped shoulders and a frown? Or with your shoulders lifted and a smile because you're excited about what you're doing? I happen to know that you're passionate about being a leader and being a success in business. How do I know? Because you're reading this book. You have a passion for learning and improving yourself. That is HUGE.

I don't live in a fairy tale. I understand it's not always possible to be passionate about everything we do. For example, it's not easy to be passionate about sitting on a crowded bus for your commute.

However, you might strike up a conversation with the person next to you and make a new friend on your commute. You might not love your job, but when you get home, you love cooking! That's passion. And you can work on being more passionate about your job. Or, maybe you're working on developing your passion into an entrepreneurial idea. Or maybe that person on the crowded bus calls you and says that her company has a job opening, are you interested? I understand you only have so much passion, and may have to parcel it out. That's fine, but be aware of your level of passion, your enthusiasm, and your eagerness. And if you want to be a leader, watch how your passion turns you into the pied piper. **People want to be led by passionate people.**

Now let's talk about **passion for how you do things.** Perhaps you are currently working at a job or career you don't love with joy, eagerness, and enthusiasm. Maybe you're the person that puts the screws into the doors of cars on an assembly line. It may not be the most exciting job, but do you do it with passion? Do you do it correctly, properly, perfectly every time? That's passion. Someday someone is going to count on the fact that you screwed that door on perfectly and it held up in an accident. Because you were passionate about what you do, you may have saved a life.

Perhaps you repair computers and to you it's just every day work. Guess what, if you repair my computer, you just saved my life! Imagine how you affect a customer's life by repairing that computer properly or not. It may be just a job to you, but to the customer, it's everything. So do everything you do with passion!

Even if you don't love what you do, you can be passionate about:

- Doing a good job
- Taking responsibility for the work you do
- Working as a team with your co-workers
- Becoming an effective leader

Even if you hate your job, you can be passionate about doing those things.

Live your life with passion. Passion, like fear, is contagious. Passionate people inspire others to be passionate. Be the one who inspires! Be the leader.

This goes for your home life, your work life, yourself, how you interact with friends, family, and co-workers. Leap out of bed to see the sunrise, go for a walk in the rain, and sing in the shower. How often have you heard anybody complain that someone was too passionate about life? Not very often because dull is out, passion is in! So many people mistake passion for quitting their job and trying to go it on their own. But if you love what you do, and/or do it with passion, then you don't necessarily have to do things on your own. You can still have the entrepreneurial spirit and work with others. And when you allow yourself to be passionate you'll be amazed as to how others pick up on it and follow your lead.

Dale Carnegie said, "Today is life—the only life you are sure of. Make the most of today. Let the winds of enthusiasm sweep through you. Live today with gusto."

Specifically, here are some things you can do to live with more passion. I believe there are four elements to living with passion and if you improve these elements, you'll raise the level of passion in your life: **Love, Giving, Laughter, and Tears.** When you live with these four elements, you will live as a passionate person—others will see you as passionate—and they'll follow you.

Love

This is not a book about dating or about your personal life, but there's more to love than that. When I speak about love, sure, it's about how much love you give to your partner, your family, and your friends. But did you ever think about how much love you give your co-workers and your customers? Do you show love for those people? I don't mean via diamond rings. One of the ways we showed our customers we cared about them was simply by remembering their birthdays and sending a hand-signed card in the mail. You remember the mail, don't you? Love means caring deeply, and people, whether they are your family or your customers, know whether or not you love them. I understand, and there are some co-workers, or others in your life, and even some customers you don't love. Believe me, I understand. It's a matter of effort and where you direct it. But remember the more love you give, the more it will come back to you.

Giving

Be generous to your clients. Giving is important in your personal and business life. When a client feels you gave generously, they're more likely to become a raving fan.

What gives you more excitement and joy: receiving or giving gifts? If you think about that, you will invariably remember it's more fun to give than to get—because it is. There's nothing quite like seeing somebody's eyes light up as they open a gift from you.

NAVIGATING ENTREPRENEURSHIP

*The joy and importance of giving is surprisingly important to the way
you feel about yourself.*

When you give, without expecting anything in return, it feels good.
And you make others feel good, which makes you feel good and it
becomes self-perpetuating.

When the enormous tsunami hit Phuket, Thailand, we collected a
relief fund from friends and family. Upon our return to Thailand, we
delivered this money to the 12 workers in the boat yard who were working on our boat. We effectively gave each worker more than three months
wages to help get them back on their feet. One worker had lost his wife,
another his home, and the others had lost at least one person close to
them. We were looked upon as saviors, and all we did was give them some
money. It was easy for us to raise the money compared to what they had
been through, and the result meant so much to them. Giving is so easy.
And it comes back to you many times over.

When we were anchored in Zihuatanejo, Mexico, we heard on the
radio that some other sailors were in need of fresh drinking water. Aboard
JULIA, we had plenty of water because we had a fresh watermaker we ran
every day. We radioed Brad and Laura to come over and bring all their
water containers. They came, we became fast friends, and are still good
friends with them today—all for just a few gallons of water.

*In business, you can give by under-promising and over-delivering to
your co-workers and customers.*

Giving is the real joy in life. It provides the satisfaction missing from
material goods. Give more than you promise. Give for no other reason than
it benefits someone else without expecting anything in return. This alone
will bring you more business and loyal customers than you ever imagined.

Laughing and Crying

I put them in the same category because they are so similar in their positive effect on you. While sailing around the world, and before that, while
spending 20 years in a business career that took me on an emotional roller
coaster as wild as any storm in the ocean, I learned that laughter and

tears were a source of joy and cleansing. You've all heard the expression, "Laughter is the best medicine," and I agree with that. Even when something seems so bad that you really just want to cry, sometimes it's better just to laugh at the absurdity of it all.

While in Indonesia, we had so many big mechanical failures and problems getting replacement parts, I really wanted to cry. But we all know there's no crying in sailing, so what could I do? Laugh! Laughing is more fun anyway and if you laugh hard enough, your sides hurt and that makes you laugh more, and then the people around you start laughing and before you know it, everybody is laughing at a ridiculous situation.

Have you ever stood at the gate waiting to board your airplane and watched them post the "delayed" sign? First it says delayed by 10 minutes and you figure *Okay no problem*. Then it changes to 30 minutes, and you think, *I'll have to move quickly to make my connection*. Then they post delayed by an hour or two hours and you realize that not only are you going to miss your connecting flight, but also you're going to miss your business dinner or appointment. Or maybe you won't be able to get any sleep before your presentation first thing in the morning. What do you do here; cry? No, of course not. You laugh, call the client and explain, and the client understands and laughs with you. And while you may not be thrilled with the result, you learn to laugh it off. Crying wouldn't have helped. Laughter helped.

Learn to Laugh at Yourself

I find some of the best entertainment around comes from laughing at myself. I frequently catch myself doing silly and stupid things and find them an endless source of amusement. Instead of being defensive about making mistakes, learn to laugh at them!

Leaders learn to laugh, especially at themselves.

Crying Is Cleansing

In cultures where crying is seen as losing face, people are attending group cry sessions because they are so cleansing. Missing an appointment is one thing, losing a loved one is a different type of loss. The first you can laugh at. The second deserves lots of good crying, pouring out of tears, wallowing in the sadness for as long as it takes to get through it. That's life. That is how we are built. That is what we are supposed to do and anybody who has ever told you different is trying to put up an artificial barrier that has no valid basis other than maybe what he or she were taught. So when it's time to cry—go for it. It's human. Leaders learn to cry.

Through the laughter and the tears, leaders are at the same time working on solutions to fix problems. You might be laughing at missing your flight, but you're working on re-booking another. And you may be crying over a dramatic loss, but you're looking to the future—to the day when you will be through crying. **Leaders look forward.**

Living with passion will drive you through any fears or obstacles that stand in your way of achieving your dreams. My passion to sail around the world first surfaced at age 13 when I found my first sailboat in a garbage dumpster. I remember feeling the passion. I got butterflies in my stomach, my heart skipped a beat, for I had discovered my passion. I kept that passion alive for 33 years before beginning my sailing trip around the world. During that six-year odyssey, there were many opportunities to turn around and give up, but my passion kept me going. I freely admit that I am a passionate person and I love living like this. **I hope I am giving you the gift of igniting your passion because it will make you a success.**

MOST COMMON MISTAKE: Thinking that these vital elements to life of love, laughter, and tears are less important to your success than hard work and stress.

Action Guide

For three days, write down something you did to bring more love into your life. It could be hugging or calling someone.

Laugh about something, anything. And if you need to cry, do it.

Do something passionate: Cook a new meal, walk in the rain, splash in a puddle, create art, write, anything that makes you feel passionate. Make a mental note of the satisfying feelings you receive.

Regarding giving, do I really need to give you an exercise to practice giving? Okay, practice giving. Give little things, give big things, and give whatever you can to whomever. For example, if it's your habit to walk by homeless people. Try stopping and giving them $5. Not a quarter, but rather $5 or more. And watch their eyes light up. It'll make your day, and imagine what it will do for them.

CHAPTER 11

Leading Others Effectively

Being an entrepreneur often means beginning a small business by yourself, and almost all of what you have read so far has been about understanding how to lead yourself.

However, when you achieve a level of success that requires others to join in your venture, you will need to be the leader of them as well. So let's talk about leading others. I could just say, "Take all of what you have already learned in this book about leading yourself and apply it to leading others." Tempting … but no, because there are differences between leading yourself and leading others. And, there are more elements to consider when leading others so I'm going to go into some depth here. I'm going to make a lot of points of which many could be a chapter unto themselves.

For some, leading others is easier than leading yourself. For others, leading themselves is easier. At least when you are leading yourself, you only have one type of personality to deal with—yours.

When leading others, there are multiple personalities involved and you must consider that everybody is not just like you.

And isn't that a good thing! I certainly wouldn't want everyone to be like me—that would be boring. An old Afghan saying says, "If you think you are leading and no one is following, you are just taking a walk." Let's ensure you're not just taking a walk.

Let's start with breaking a few of my pet peeve myths about leadership. We're going to focus on the positive and good leadership skills … but I just have to get these out of the way and off my chest.

First of all, leading is not telling or yelling. It is not abusing your authority and treating workers as underlings. It's not saying, "This is how we will do something" without at least some involvement from those you are leading. Now remember I'm writing for entrepreneurs in the business world. You might be a one or two-person company or a mid-size company, or you might be a CEO who is entrepreneurial-minded. My point is, we're not talking about the military where if the General says to run up a hill, you have to run up that hill and you have no say in the matter. I wanted to be sure we were clear on that.

Secondly, leading is not making decisions without gathering information. That's dictatorship. Leading IS consulting, facilitating, asking, gathering information, and then when all of the information possible about a subject is garnered, leadership is making a decision. On my boat sailing around the world, I almost always asked my crew where they thought we should anchor in a bay. Even if I already knew where I wanted to anchor, I would ask. Then we would motor slowly through the anchorage letting everybody gather their own information. We'd have a quickie melding of the minds, and then I would make the final decision, because in the end, the leader does make the final decision. On a boat, that is of course emphasized dramatically and the captain's word is final. But I believe if there's time, and it's not a panic situation, why not get as much information as you can? That's what a true leader does. Sometimes that information comes from people and sometimes it comes from other sources of information.

Leadership is making decisions after listening and gathering information. I often had my mind changed by information I didn't see at first until offered by one of my crew. Being a good leader means getting information from others and being open to accepting that information. Why wouldn't you want more and better information than you have already?

The trap that many leaders fall into is their own ego. Don't feel as though by making a decision on your own, you will earn more respect. It's the other way around. When you consider the input from others and listen, you will gain instant respect.

Recognize the opinions of others, acknowledge their contribution, and politely override them if you like.

You were given two ears and only one mouth for a reason: You should listen twice as much as you speak. John F. Kennedy was famous for having cabinet members he felt were smarter than he was in each of their special areas. He listened, took their advice to heart, and in the end made the hard decisions by himself based on all of the information he had available. That's leadership.

As captain, I always had an open-door policy and told my crew they would never get in trouble for waking me or asking a question no matter how small or silly they thought it might be. One night, one of my crew woke me up swearing that we were going to hit a ship. "Look! I can see the lights," she said. "There's the stern light and there's the light on the top of the ship's cabin!" I had to agree, it sure did look like a ship, so I said, "Let's see if we can find that ship on the radar." There was nothing but an empty screen. As we watched the "ship" for a few minutes, we saw it rise above the horizon and show itself: a crescent moon with its two points coming up over the horizon! But it didn't bother me I had been awakened, because what if it had been a ship? Then for sure I would have wanted to be awake. Plus, I got a great story to tell!

Mutually agreed-upon solutions are very popular in entrepreneurial companies. Most people working around you are also bright independent thinkers, so take advantage of that. Start by trusting cooperation rather than competition. Everything doesn't have to be a contest. Remember that everyone adds value, and everyone has the right to their opinions, even if you think they are wrong. You've been wrong before too!

Please don't misinterpret what I'm saying. There is a time and place for the leader to say, "This is it." When the wind comes up at sea, one way to deal with it is to "reef" or reduce the size of your sails. Common seamanship knowledge goes like this: "If you're thinking about reefing, you should have already done it." There's no time for a meeting, or to take in the opinion of everybody onboard. You have every right as captain to announce, "All hands on deck. Prepare to reef!" When a good crew hears that, they will be on deck within 30 seconds and there will never be a question. Ever. They know that you know something they don't, and you are looking out for their safety.

And remember that leaders must make the final decision. When leading others, don't fall into decision-making traps such as procrastination or making no decision. Remember what you learned about leading yourself; making no decision IS a decision.

My third pet peeve is thinking that leadership is pointing out what is wrong. Rather, a good leader points out what is right. Praise and critique are both important. As you look for the good around you when leading yourself, look for the good in others. Make people happy by giving compliments, thanking them for a job well done. And if you have more than just one person in your company, do it in front of others. Everybody wants to be praised and the highest form of recognition is to receive it in front of others.

The fourth myth is that some people think leadership is doing everything yourself. Not true. Leadership is delegating. For the entrepreneur in many of us, delegation is one of the most difficult challenges. Theodore Roosevelt said, "The best executive is the one who has sense enough to pick good people to do what they want done, and self-restraint enough to keep from meddling with them while they do it."

Letting go of doing detailed work is easier if you stack the deck in your favor by ensuring the work will be done properly. To that goal, assign roles based on a person's:

- Strengths
- Passion
- Skills
- Temperament
- Desire for that role

Provide proper training so when you give someone a job, you know they have the skill to handle it. If not, you're just stacking the deck against their success. If it's a big role, you now know how to break that big job down into smaller achievable goals. Help the person you are giving a job to, by showing them milestones they can reach and how it will ease their stress.

Once you assign a role, let go and trust the person who is now working on this project. Demonstrate your trust by not looking over their shoulder every minute. When you assign work to someone, let them own it. That doesn't mean you can't follow up or ask how it's going, but remember it's **their** job.

Okay, that's enough negatives and myth busting of my pet peeves. I prefer to focus on the positive and what leadership IS. **Leadership is being a good communicator** and using your communication skills to help others do their job. No matter how you are communicating, be it e-mail, hand signals, or in speech, communicate with the following:

1. Respect and friendliness. Has it ever benefited you to yell at the airline ticket agent?
2. Integrity. Mean what you say and believe in what you say.
3. Be intentional. What do you want to see happen as a result of the communication?
4. Be organized. Don't ramble. Don't repeat points unless they're truly worth repeating, unless they're that critical. And then for emphasis say, "Let me repeat that." A summary is different than repeating. Do summarize.
5. Clarity. Leave no doubt about what you mean. Be simple, use few words.
6. Timeliness. Don't put off answering anyone's e-mail, phone call, or certainly a customer's inquiry.
7. Anticipate questions and objections. Show you have thought this through.

Imagine if you had to communicate underwater with nothing but hand signals. If you're a scuba diver, you already know about this form of communication. There are hand signals to communicate what depth you're going to, how much air you have left, how long you'll stay at a particular safety depth on the way back up, did you see that lobster? did you see that shark? I'm cold, I'm out of air, and can I use yours? I want to go up, let's swim over there, and it goes on. The interesting thing about diving is that because you never dive alone, (although those of you who have read my book, **The Boy Behind the Gate** know that I broke that rule once and nearly died as a result), but back to never diving alone, both parties have to agree on every question or statement. Let's say you're diving along a beautiful reef wall at 30 feet and your buddy wants to go down to 45 feet. You don't want to because your ears are troubling you that day.

You have to—with respect, but very clearly signal no, you want to stay at 30 feet. There's a signal for ear trouble and your buddy must respect that and stay with you at 30 feet. It's a system of forced cooperation that works. Be sure to use that clarity, respect, organization, and intention in your everyday dealings with others when leading.

Anchoring a boat has huge challenges. It's not uncommon to hear couples yelling at each other from the back of the boat to the front and vice versa about where they should anchor, how much chain to put out, and the miscommunications and arguments are a common source of hilarious entertainment to those already anchored in that area. While sailing around the world, Ken and I never yelled. In fact, we never spoke during the anchoring process. And we were known to be those amazing two guys who could anchor under any conditions without a spoken word. How'd we do it? Hand signals. Brevity, clarity, and timeliness were critical.

Then there was a communication issue I had to put a stop to early in the journey. When I would give an order, some crew would respond, "OK." For example, while hoisting the mainsail, I might announce, "Prepare to hoist the main." The response from a crew must be clear as to their readiness or intentions. So, I might hear back, "Standby, not ready," or "Ready to hoist." However, "OK" didn't tell me anything. It was unclear and vague. Therefore I had to change what I expected. I said that I no longer wanted to hear, "OK," but rather "Ready, Not ready," or "Can I go to the bathroom first?" Anything but "OK."

Here's a story you may have heard before and it's a great reminder of how important clarity of communication can be. One dark and stormy night off the east coast, a U.S. aircraft carrier received a radio call from the Canadians.

>Canadians: "Please divert your course 15 degrees to the south to avoid collision."
>Americans: "Recommend you divert your course 15 degrees to the north to avoid a collision."
>Canadians: "Negative. You will have to divert your course 15 degrees to the south to avoid a collision."
>Americans: "This is the captain of a US Naval warship. I say again, divert YOUR course."

Canadians: "No, I say again, divert YOUR course."

Americans: "This is the aircraft carrier USS Lincoln, the second largest ship in the United States' Atlantic fleet. We are accompanied by three destroyers, three cruisers and numerous support vessels. I demand you change your course 15 degrees north—I say again, that's one-five degrees north—or counter-measures will be undertaken to ensure the safety of this ship."

Canadians: "This is a lighthouse. It's your call."

Leaders communicate clearly.

I briefly mentioned this before but I want to elaborate on **job responsibilities and training.** Leaders understand what they are asking others to do. Why did General George Patton stand at the front lines? Doesn't that seem a bit dangerous for a general? Yes it was, but to Patton, the positive results far outweighed the risk. Patton's now legendary 3rd army saw that he was willing to take the same risks and do any job he was asking of his soldiers. That's a very powerful demonstration and is largely responsible for driving the 3rd army to an incredible series of victories in Europe.

As captain, I never asked any crew to do a job I hadn't done. That included cleaning out the toilet pipes, climbing the mast, and every other dirty job on the boat. I also made sure that before asking a crew to do something, they were properly trained. **In the middle of a storm is not the time to train your crew how to change sails.** As a leader, you are responsible for ensuring proper training of your team.

> *When someone is properly trained, and knows they are doing a job their leader is willing to do, they feel they can do it too.*

If you don't understand what your co-workers are going through because you haven't done their job, then you are responsible for asking them how they're doing, if they have the proper training, what they need in order to accomplish the job, and if there are any problem they are experiencing.

As a leader, you must show care, understanding, and discipline. In the last point about not asking someone to do something you wouldn't, that shows understanding. However, you must also demand discipline. I have stood my share of watches at night in the cold and I understand how hard it is. Yet as captain, I still demanded that crew stand their full watch. That's being understanding, empathetic, and running a disciplined ship. If you set a deadline for a report, there better be an awfully good reason for a delay … and I don't think, "My dog ate the report," works anymore with electronic documents.

Everything is not a crisis. Don't let campfires become forest fires. Don't make a mountain out of a molehill. If you can defuse a situation or solve a problem simply, then do it. Leaders have to make more decisions than followers. It comes with the territory. Recognize this is part of your role as leader, and keep your company as crisis-free as possible. Stamping out little issues before they spread allows people to focus on their job without worry. This could be defusing a potential crisis between workers. Address it early, swiftly, and efficiently.

Anticipate problems, obstacles, and changes that are coming. You learned to do this for yourself in earlier chapters. Now you have to anticipate for everybody, for the whole company, for the whole team. Is that possible? Of course not, but you have to give it your best shot. Especially with respect to change, you must be quick to react and you must look for places where you can be proactive rather than reactive.

Be knowledgeable. If you demonstrate that you know what you're talking about, you will be respected and followed.

See the big picture. Have a plan. Just like for yourself, you must see your company or organization's vision. And that vision must be shared with everybody. Remember that a ship without a course will just meander around the oceans drifting with the wind and current. Your vision, your corporate motto, or mission statement is what you steer by and what you believe in. If everybody is working toward the same goal, you have a much better chance of achieving it.

Taking credit. Or rather, not taking credit, but giving credit. When you are doing a good job as leader and something is achieved, those who did the work should feel they did it themselves. They don't even know they were led, and a good leader doesn't care about taking the credit. He or she gives the credit to those who did the job. If you're a coaching client of mine, I don't remind you, "I told you so," or "See, why didn't you believe me?" All I did was point you in the right direction. I offer the credit to you that YOU are the one who made the achievement. As a leader, when things work well, give the credit away.

A good leader is confident enough to set their ego aside.

Unfortunately, when things don't go well, you also have to take the credit. As captain of a boat, you are responsible for everything that happens on that boat. Everything means the good and the bad. As an entrepreneurial leader, you too are responsible for everything that happens. You might have an employee who messes something up. Doesn't matter, it was your fault. The leader is always responsible for what happens. It goes with the territory, that's just the way it is. Every good leader owns up to this responsibility. In my many years of business, I have seen so many so-called leaders blame others that I wonder how they became the leader in the first place. Don't be afraid to take the fall. What good does it do to blame someone else? Most likely they didn't have proper training, motivation, or enthusiasm—and these are all your responsibility.

Accept feedback and critique as well as you give it. First of all, you don't know everything. So if someone gives you feedback and critique, instead of being defensive, why not listen? It doesn't mean they're right or wrong, but their opinion or critique might have validity and help you. It's like a free analysis!

And when you give feedback and critique, there are times for sugar coating, and there are times for no sugar. But in my opinion, there is never a time for yelling. It's not needed and it's not effective. Studies show over and over that when someone raises their voice, listeners close their ears, so try toning it down.

Be methodical about what you say, organized as to how you say it, and most importantly, offer and show how to do something better the next time. Good leaders get people to follow them because they have something to offer. Harsh criticism at high volume will get you nowhere.

Here are five secrets to motivate people depending on where they're at in their lives. People are different. They have unique personalities and are at various levels of achievement in their lives so their needs are different. Have you ever heard of Maslow's Hierarchy of Needs? You would have probably studied about Abraham Maslow in your first and for most of us, only college psychology class, Psych 101. Maslow's findings show what makes people tick and the psychology world has pretty much agreed on his **Hierarchy of Needs.** It basically describes what we need, what we want, and what ultimately satisfies us.

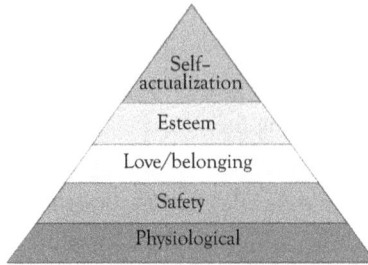

Our first basic needs are physiological: air, food, water, clothing, shelter, and safety. So first you have to be sure your co-workers are paid enough to live a basic decent life. To make this clearer, I'm going to describe the incentive award that would motivate this person. In this case, it would be cash to pay for food and rent.

Once physiological needs are satisfied, people look for safety such as personal and financial security, health and well-being. The incentive that would fit here would be job security, health benefits, and a savings plan.

The third level of Maslow's Hierarchy of Needs is love, belonging, and social acceptance. Social acceptance is provided by intimacy with friends, family, and connections with others such as those with whom we work. Everybody wants to feel like they belong. They want to interact with their friends, family, and co-workers. Teamwork satisfies this need well as it gives a sense of worth when all are participating. The incentive award that would fit here might be a new television set to show off to the family and friends, and membership in a club, or company social group.

Self-esteem is what we strive for next in our quest for a life of satisfaction and purpose. It is an affirmation of how one feels about oneself. Do they command respect from others, are they valuable, are their contributions heard, have they reached a certain level of competence? The right incentive award would be making sales goal and being invited on the President's Club trip.

And lastly comes self-actualization, which a person achieves when facing challenges (not necessarily overcoming them), when they recognize their real purpose, and when they succeed in reaching their full potential. It is a place of great self-fulfillment when one feels they have reached a place of success. This is the feeling people get from teaching, from helping others, from climbing Mt. Everest, and from sailing around the world. (Although I have a long way to go before I feel true self-fulfillment, I feel the most self-actualized when helping others as in writing this book). Either way, it is a level of achievement for which I will continue to strive. The incentive award for these people would be making sales goal and being invited to speak to the rest of the group at the President's Club trip.

Now you know what makes people tick, from the bottom of human needs to the top. How do you build solutions to these human needs into your daily business life for yourself and your company? I could spend hours on this, so if you feel you need more information on this subject, feel free to contact me.

Try a variety of campaigns such as surveys from customers, nominations from co-workers, and incentive programs for sales. These are the big loud programs visible to everyone.

You can be subtler like talk loudly enough in the hallway so a person's co-workers hear you praise that person. Watch how fast the praise flies around the water cooler.

Recognition, recognition, recognition. From putting someone's photo on a bulletin board to highlighting them in the online company or customer newsletter, people swell with pride when praised for doing a good job.

Manage by walking around. This applies whether you are captain of a boat and walking around the deck asking how people are, to walking the halls and cubicles.

Ask, and listen! Make each person feel as though they are the reason for the success of the company and that you couldn't do it without them. And you couldn't.

That was a fun little sidetrack on what makes people tick, but let's get back to leading others. Your positive emotions count. I don't know of an emotion that is not contagious, so your outward emotions that your co-workers and customers see are critical. They are watching.

First of all, **Confidence** is what followers look for in a leader. Are you confident your plan will succeed? If not, are you at least showing outward confidence? Of course you have some doubts that others won't, because you're the leader. You have more information than they do. When we were caught in that horrible storm in the Red Sea, I was more scared than my crew. Why? Because I knew the downside potential. I knew what could happen to us better than they did. I was more aware of the weather, the size of the seas, the equipment that could break, and the overall danger to the boat and us. But I didn't show it. I showed I was captain, and that I was confident. The last thing I needed was for them to think I didn't have confidence in our skill or equipment. I had to show confidence we were going to survive.

It was the same when the Gulf War broke out and our company was on the verge of collapse. I carried myself with confidence we would succeed in our new plan of providing merchandise awards instead of travel.

People are looking up to you. Think about what they see. If you're unsure, they'll be unsure.

Secondly, are you **enthusiastic**? Do you show up on time or early every day? Or do you just show up once in a while and expect everyone else to be there every day? Are you a team supporter? Are you upbeat, enthusiastic, eager, keen, and on fire? Do you share that enthusiasm? Do you share good news with your co-workers? And perhaps consider not sharing all the bad news. Robert Louis Stevenson said, "Keep your fears to yourself, but share your courage with others." Your job is to motivate people, to lead them. Keep them upbeat!

And of course, remain passionate. Share your passion for success, for your product, for customer service, for people, and for quality with your team, your co-workers, your crew, and your customers.

Your passion for the highest level of service is contagious and will spread throughout your company and your industry. Leaders show and share their passion and therefore inspire others. Remember to be the one who inspires.

And lastly, **be humble**. Nobody likes a braggart. Nobody likes to hear someone talk only about him or herself.

MOST COMMON MISTAKE: The most common mistake made when leading others is thinking you're the boss. You're not the boss. You're the leader. And I'm sure that by now in this book, you have learned to recognize the difference.

Action Guide

The whole chapter is an action guide. I humbly suggest that you re-read this entire chapter again tomorrow.

CHAPTER 12

Choosing to Lead Is Choosing to Succeed

The final chapter in this book is short, and it is **the single most important trait to being a leader.** Sometimes we are thrust into positions of leadership without our approval. That does happen. It could be in an emergency situation like in the Poseidon Adventure where you must lead everyone to safety. Or you could have been promoted as a surprise, not expecting it, and now find yourself in a position of leadership wondering how you can be a better leader.

But more likely, you were expecting the promotion, or you wanted the promotion, or you started your own company, or any number of scenarios in which you CHOSE to lead. Whether or not you are in a leadership position of your own doing or someone else's doing, it is still your choice what you do with the position. You **do** get to choose (unless you're still leading people to safety on the Poseidon).

The fact that you are choosing to lead is the single most important trait to becoming an effective leader. When you choose to lead, you choose to accept the responsibilities that go with it, which includes putting your heart into it.

Choosing to lead will make you perform better in all of the areas you've read about in this book. You will stand up tall, thrust your shoulders back and say, "I'm a leader."

Some say leaders are born, not made. I don't buy it. Leaders aren't born, they are made, and a big part of being made is choosing to lead. You have that choice. If you feel differently, that you just don't have what it takes to lead, then you have to work harder at learning to lead by following the keys you've learned in this book. I'll admit that to some, leading is more natural than it is to others. If it doesn't seem to come natural to you, it will take a bit more learning. Review this book again. It's in your hands and it won't expire after one read. You get to read it as many times as you want.

You can start your goals over as many times as you want. You can have a fresh look at the Action Guide and do the exercises starting from the beginning if you want. You can read other books about leadership and entrepreneurship. You can bring me in as a personal or a company coach, and of course you'll find me at www.larryjacobson.com. You have lots of options. The point is:

Whether you feel you were born to lead or you are learning to lead, if you choose to lead, you can.

"Leadership is letting go of tasks while retaining responsibility for everything that happens." Who said that quote? I did. Larry Jacobson

CHAPTER 13

Quick Review

As an entrepreneur or one who is entrepreneurial-minded, you are some-one who thrives on the challenges you face. You're a dreamer and you're willing to take the risks necessary to make your dreams come true. You're willing to accept change and your fears. You have tenacity, passion, and choose to stay with your challenging life choices. You accept the challenge of improving yourself and you're willing or even eager to lead others. To be a successful entrepreneur, you recognize the importance of leadership. It's an exciting way of life and you wouldn't have it any other way.

Let's have one last quick review of all 11 points. Leaders:

1. Dream and have vision
2. Set goals
3. Take risks
4. Are decisive and know their priorities
5. Expect and accept change
6. Manage their fears
7. Know they can learn while doing
8. Have perseverance
9. Have passion
10. Know how to lead others
11. Choose to lead

You have come a long way by completing this book toward being the leader you want to be. I hope that you'll read the entire book over again so these keys become part of your everyday way of thinking. If there's any way at all that I can support your efforts, please get in touch with me. You'll find me at www.larryjacobson.com

Here's to your Success as an Entrepreneur and as a Leader. Thank you for reading, and I'll see you at the top!

Action Guide

1. Dreaming

Here is the place to write down your big dream. Put in some details, the sand dripping between your toes, the stockholders applauding their CEO, you name it.

All effective leaders use visioning to see themselves achieving their dreams and goals.

MY BIG DREAM

```



```

DETAILS OF MY BIG DREAM

```




```

2. Goals and Priorities

This is the longest section in the Action Guide, but it's important because it builds your foundation. The rest will grow out of this: Let's try to help you figure out what you want and let's do it by category:

FINANCIAL
How much money you want to make, what investments you would like, what about real estate, savings?

PERSONAL
What would you like to see in a Relationship—maybe you don't have one, and want one. Maybe you're in one, and want to get out. What about your health such as your weight, eating habits, exercise? Add material things you want such as beach house, sailboat, new car, new set of dishes, a bicycle?

CAREER
Are you Happy? Do you want a new direction? New promotion, switch to a new company, start a business? Sometimes Career and Financial overlap. If they do for you, that's fine. But for some, your current career doesn't coincide with your financial goals. Only you can assess that.

Now look at the timeframe for each category and each goal:

What do you want financially, personally, and with your career over?

- x 6 months
- x 1 year
- x 5 years
- x 10 years

Don't complicate this, just do it. Once you've written your goals down, and they can be one word, then write down three action items needed to accomplish each goal. This may take a bit of time, be patient, and keep at it. Really think out each step and write them down. These can include things that you need to do, people you need to help you, or skills you need to learn. For example, if you want to write a book, but can't type, it might be helpful to learn… or, to buy the software that translates your voice into the written word. Or, you can record your book and send it to someone and they'll type it for you. There's more than one way to get something done! It's so easy for all of us to come up with reasons not to do things. Sometimes we have to tell ourselves: No excuses.

Now label these action items by their priority. We'll talk more about priorities later, but for now, just label them with an A for higher priority, B for next, and so on.

3. Taking Risks

For each goal you have, write down a risk you'll have to take in order to pursue the action steps you have listed. Identify any risks as you see them. They can be very simple. For example, if you want to open that bakery we discussed, the risk would be missing your kids' Saturday morning soccer games.

Now you have to ask yourself "am I willing to take that risk?" and write down your answer. Committing your answer to paper can have a very powerful effect on your attitude about the risk when it's staring you in the eye. If you said that you were willing to take the risk and you put it on paper, it's going to be easier to do.

Personal Goals

Priority	Personal Goals	Action Steps	Risks of Goal or Action Steps	Priority of Goal or Action Step	Take Risk?
6 MONTHS					☐ Yes ☐ No
1 YEAR					☐ Yes ☐ No
5 YEARS					☐ Yes ☐ No
10 YEARS					☐ Yes ☐ No

Financial Goals

Priority	Financial Goals	Action Steps	Risks of Goal or Action Steps	Priority of Goal or Action Step	Take Risk?
6 MONTHS					☐ Yes ☐ No
1 YEAR					☐ Yes ☐ No
5 YEARS					☐ Yes ☐ No
10 YEARS					☐ Yes ☐ No

Career Goals

Priority	Career Goals	Action Steps	Risks of Goal or Action Steps	Priority of Goal or Action Step	Take Risk?
6 MONTHS					☐ Yes ☐ No
1 YEAR					☐ Yes ☐ No
5 YEARS					☐ Yes ☐ No
10 YEARS					☐ Yes ☐ No

4. Making Decisions

Go back to your goals and set priorities next to them A–D. Your priorities will guide you in so many decisions, so take your time, and think about them.

The next exercise is to practice making decisions.

Here's how to practice making decisions and demonstrate to yourself that you are a decisive person. Write down three things you have been considering doing or not doing. I don't care what they are, big or small. It could be what you're going to prepare for lunch. Now DECIDE on those three things. I mean NOW. Right Now. There! Done! You're decisive. Once you've made the decisions, tell yourself that you're decisive. Look at you: you made a decision.

Do this three days in a row.

Practice sticking to your decisions. It will make you a more decisive person. You will learn to trust in your decisions.

DAY ONE
I've been considering doing:

1. _____

2. _____

3. _____

DAY TWO
I've been considering doing:

1. _____

2. _____

3. _____

DAY THREE

I've been considering doing:

1. _____

2. _____

3. _____

5. Expecting and Accepting Change

Proactively change something very small in your life today. Change your drink, change something that you eat, change something that you wear. Change your blouse, your shirt, change your socks, I don't care, just change something and recognize that you proactively did it.

Three things I changed proactively:

1. _____

2. _____

3. _____

The next exercise is going to take some more awareness on your part. I want you to react to something that changes and be okay with it.

Three reactions I changed:

1. _____

2. _____

3. _____

6. Fear

Write down one thing you are afraid of doing, seeing, or experiencing.

Under that, write the three elements that make you afraid of it.

I am afraid of

_____

I am afraid of this because:

1. _____

2. _____

3. _____

Next, provide the solution to those fears:

1. _____

2. _____

3. _____

Recognize and embrace your fears. Remember that they make you focused on the task at hand; they make you sharp and alert. And you can use those fears to your advantage.

7. Do Something New Today

Something you don't already know how to do. It could be a new exercise in the gym. It could be looking for a virtual assistant online. You could try writing a short three-line poem. How about writing your company mission statement or rewriting it. Today, I did this, and it was new to me:

```



```

Learn something new. I don't care what it is. Your goal here is to prove to yourself that you can learn something new. Today, I learned this, and it was new to me:

```



```

8. Perseverance

Looking back at your goals, where will you need strength and perseverance? Staying power? With just your top three goals, write down what type of strength you're going to need. Emotional, physical, new skill sets, practice of your art or presentation, patience, someone else to do it for you?

Goal #1 _____

Strength I'm going to need _____

Goal #2 _____

Strength I'm going to need _____

Goal #3 _____

Strength I'm going to need _____

9. Passion

For three days, write down one thing you did to bring more passion into your life.

1. _____

2. _____

3. _____

Don't forget to give! It'll make both giver and receiver feel so good!

10. Leading Others

Re-read to Chapter 10 and take notes here:

11. Choose to Lead!

Repeat to yourself: I choose to lead. I choose to lead. I choose to lead. I choose to lead.

Congratulations! You have now begun to navigate the choppy waters of leadership. It takes practice and experience. Use these 11 proven keys the way we have discussed them and your leadership skills will soar! For questions, you'll find me at www.larryjacobson.com

And, don't forget to go to the website, http://larryjacobson.com/passion-quiz/ and download your free Passion Quiz.

©Larry Jacobson

About the Author

Larry Jacobson, Entrepreneur & Leadership Coach, a sought-after and seasoned leadership and business coach, personal life-planning coach, and speaking coach, Jacobson uses his success in business and achieving his personal dream of sailing around the world as a model to help his clients reach their goals. His experience has attracted clients from entrepreneurs, to CEOs, to public figures. Through coaching, motivational speaking, and publications, he teaches the skills, traits, and characteristics needed to achieve great accomplishments in one's business and personal life. In addition to the importance of having a vision and setting goals for achievement, he speaks with credibility from experience about managing fear, takings risks, decision making, perseverance, and his favorite subjects of passion and leadership.

A California native, circumnavigator, and adventurer, Larry Jacobson grew up on the beaches of the Pacific Ocean sailing, kayaking, swimming, and scuba diving. A graduate of the University of California at Irvine, and Berkeley, he became a nationally recognized entrepreneur with 20 years in the business world.

An avid sailor, he has over 50,000 blue water miles under his keel and authored the six-time award-winning memoir of his circumnavigation in the book, *The Boy Behind the Gate*. He lives in the San Francisco Bay Area and welcomes new friends and inquiries at: www.larryjacobson.com

Index

OTHER TITLES IN THE ENTREPRENEURSHIP AND SMALL BUSINESS MANAGEMENT COLLECTION

Scott Shane, Case Western University, Editor

- *Open Innovation Essentials for Small and Medium Enterprises: A Guide to Help Entrepreneurs in Adopting the Open Innovation Paradigm in Their Business* by Luca Escoffier, Adriano La Vopa, Phyllis Speser, and Daniel Satinsky
- *The Technological Entrepreneur's Playbook* by Ian Chaston
- *Licensing Myths & Mastery: Why Most Ideas Don't Work and What to Do About It* by William S. Seidel
- *Arts and Entrepreneurship* by J. Mark Munoz and Julie Shields
- *The Human Being's Guide to Business Growth: A Simple Process for Unleashing the Power of Your People for Growth* by Gregory Scott Chambers
- *Understanding the Family Business: Exploring the Differences Between Family and Nonfamily Businesses, Second Edition* by Keanon J. Alderson

Announcing the Business Expert Press Digital Library

Concise e-books business students need for classroom and research

This book can also be purchased in an e-book collection by your library as

- a one-time purchase,
- that is owned forever,
- allows for simultaneous readers,
- has no restrictions on printing, and
- can be downloaded as PDFs from within the library community.

Our digital library collections are a great solution to beat the rising cost of textbooks. E-books can be loaded into their course management systems or onto students' e-book readers.
The **Business Expert Press** digital libraries are very affordable, with no obligation to buy in future years. For more information, please visit **www.businessexpertpress.com/librarians**. To set up a trial in the United States, please email **sales@businessexpertpress.com**.

www.ingramcontent.com/pod-product-compliance
Lightning Source LLC
Chambersburg PA
CBHW071500200326
41519CB00019B/5810